An American in Shanghai:
Reflections on
Living in New China

**Also by Russell R. Miller**

*Snapshots: A Brief Stroll Through Asia*
East Wind Press, San Francisco, CA 2013

*Spring: Engaging Nature's Renewal in Rural Japan*
Lulu Enterprises Inc., Morrisville, NC 2007

*Singapore's Homegrown Entrepreneurs Tell You How to Do It*
Landmark Books Pte. Ltd., Singapore 2003

*Impressions*
Arion Press, San Francisco, CA 1991

*Supergrowth: Buying and Selling Agencies for Profit*
The National Underwriter Company, Cincinnati, OH 1981

**Photographs by Russell R. Miller**

*Gateway to World Religions*
AsiaPac Books Pte. Ltd., Singapore 2007

*My Singapore Story: My Heritage, My Dream*
AsiaPac Books Pte. Ltd., Singapore 2005

# AN AMERICAN IN SHANGHAI: REFLECTIONS ON LIVING IN NEW CHINA

by Russell R. Miller

米书泰

**East Wind Press**
SHANGHAI • SAN FRANCISCO

Copyright © 2013 by Russell R. Miller
Published by East Wind Press

Back cover photograph copyright © 2013 Russell R. Miller
Project Manager: Peter Beren, PeterBeren.com
Book design by Mark Shepard, ShepGraphics.com
Edited by Mary Pols

All rights reserved. No part of this publication may be produced or transmitted in any form or by any means, electronic or mechanical, including photocopy, recording or any other information storage and retrieval system without prior permission in writing from the Publisher.

    Miller, Russell R., 1937-
        An American in Shanghai : reflections on living in new China / by Russell R. Miller. -- First edition.
        pages cm.
        ISBN 978-0-9911354-0-0 (pbk.)
        ISBN 978-0-9911354-1-7 (hc)
        ISBN 978-0-9911354-7-9 (ebook)

        1. China--Description and travel. 2. Shanghai (China)--Description and travel. 3. China--Social life and customs--2002- 4. Miller, Russell R., 1937---Travel --China. 5. Americans--China--Biography. I. Title.

DS712.M55 2013        915.104'6'092
                          QBI13-200006

Third Edition

*To all those regular folks who didn't have to help an oblivious stranger yet helped me find my way down the right street, buy a subway ticket, gather some flowers, find some vegetables, take a train, or who just prevented me from making an idiot of myself.*

# Contents

Acknowledgments…9

Introduction…11

Chapter 1: Welcome to China…13

Chapter 2: Getting to Know You…17

Chapter 3: What Brought Me to China…23

Chapter 4: Shanghai Life…37

Chapter 5: City with an Incredible Past…49

Chapter 6: The Great Leap Backward…55

Chapter 7: Like Finding Your Way in a Thick Fog…59

Chapter 8: My Special Places…69

Chapter 9: Changing Seasons, Changing Clothes…79

Chapter 10: Spirit of Enterprise…93

Chapter 11: We're keeping Our Eye on You…103

Chapter 12: Religion…123

Chapter 13: Let's Eat…133

Chapter 14: Expo…141

Chapter 15: The Woman's Dilemma…145

Chapter 16: Family Life and Death…157

Chapter 17: Pollution and Epidemics…161

Chapter 18: Tale of the Three Pearls…167

Chapter 19: Social Enterprises and Nonprofits…173

And Now What?…185

Further Reading…187

# Acknowledgments

I've been in Shanghai for more than five years, and almost every day is a revelation. This society is quite different than the one I grew up with in San Francisco, so I learn something new each day. What follows are some of my reactions and reflections, primarily about Shanghai and China, but from time to time bringing in other places in a region I have been visiting and sometimes living in, for close to thirty years.

I have been lucky enough to develop some very good friends and almost universally have learned from them. One of the keenest observers is Robert A. Theleen, the founder along with his wonderful wife Jenny, of ChinaVest, a premier financial advisory and investment firm. Bob came to China in the pivotal year of 1976 and continues to live here today, respected by all who would try and find their way through the thicket of Chinese corporate opportunity. I am happy to say I've stolen several of his best stories and used them without attribution, mainly as stimulant to get him to write the book that we all know he has in him.

I also want to especially thank the indomitable Ai Ai Wong of Singapore, who encouraged me to write another book. She relit the fuse.

Many others have given me insights and encouragement including, but not only Cassie Chen, Milly Chen, Sophie Lin Yi Cheng, Wendy Ding, Gigi Feng, Xiaoming Fu, Ping Gong, Helen Dai Haiuan, Grace Huang, Hanji Huang, Vivian Li, Ting Li, Bonita Lim, Flora Lou Fen, Laura Qiu Ling Lu, Susan Lu Xiao Ni, Yun Qiao, Jane Sha, Tina Shengwei M.D., Angela Sui, Isabella Sun Shuang Yi, Connie Wang, Juquan Wang, Pearl Wang, Joanna Way, Yovia Yue Xu, Guo Xiaolei, Man Paz Zhao, Zhao Xun, Jennifer Ye, Candice Zeng, Ann Zhang, and Xiaoxiao Zhang.

I also want to thank my long-suffering editor, Mary Pols, who when handed scrambled eggs created Eggs Benedict.

I also want to acknowledge the many students from a variety of universities here and in Beijing that have listened to me and I to them, as we wrestled with understanding the emerging world with China in a leadership position.

I constantly try to read articles and books to improve my understanding of the history and development that has taken place and is taking place every day here. I hope there are not many errors perpetrated by my lack of formal training in the history and culture of China.

All footnotes, unless otherwise noted, are from Wikipedia. In many instances I've shortened or modified their text slightly to make them clearer. I have also created two fictional characters in the book to try to give some intensity to changes that were happening in their era in Shanghai. Meet Mrs. Yang and Sister Hu Li Ling.

## Introduction

Shang-Hai proper is situated on the left-hand bank of the little Wang-Poo River, which, meeting the Woosung at right-angles, joins the Yang-tse-Kiang, or Blue River, and ultimately flows into the Yellow Sea. The town is oval in shape, lying north and south, enclosed by high walls, through which five outlets lead to the suburbs. The narrow, dirty streets are little better than paved lanes; the dingy shops, without fronts or stocks to attract, are served by shopmen often naked to their waists; not a carriage nor palanquin, and very rarely even a horseman, passes by here and there are scattered a few native temples and chapels belonging to foreigners; the only places of recreation are a 'tea-garden,' and a swampy parade-ground, the dampness of which is accounted for by its being on the site of former rice-fields. Such are the chief points of a town, which, undesirable as it may seem as a place of residence, yet numbers a population of two hundred thousand, and is of considerable commercial importance.

—Jules Verne's 1883 novel, *The Tribulations of a Chinese Gentleman*

Chinese modernity was created in Shanghai. In technology and organization, in taste and style, the great city at the mouth of the Yangzi River shaped the hybrid patterns that gave meaning to modern China. Shanghai modernity was always contested. Some Chinese abhorred it because of its foreign cravings and moral perturbations, and its ability to rattle their concepts of the native, national, or original. In the imagination of leaders from the Empress Dowager to Mao Zedong, Shanghai was unclean, the great whore whom everyone moved in and out of but who belonged to no one.

—Odd Arne Westad's 2013 history *Restless Empire, China and the World Since 1750*

Shanghai is a non-productive city. It is a parasitic city. It is a criminal city. It is a refugee city. It is the paradise of adventurers.
—Shanghai newspaper, 1949, quoted in *The Search for Modern China* by Jonathan D. Spence

What does anybody here know of China?... Everything is covered by a veil, through which a glimpse of what is within may occasionally be caught, a glimpse just sufficient to set the imagination at work and more likely to mislead than to inform.
—Thomas Babington Macaulay, British secretary of state for war, in the House of Commons, April, 1840

# Chapter 1

## *Welcome to China*

In the mideighties I ventured to Japan, and in subsequent years made many visits and even established an office there. I lived and worked in Singapore for seven years, and in all that time I traveled to China only incidentally. The place I'd always thought of as a massive red blob on the map of Asia seemed confusing, unsanitary, and untidy. People jostled each other. They wouldn't wait in lines like the methodically organized citizens of Japan. They talked loudly on their cell phones. They coughed; they spat. There was air pollution and tainted food. They were *Communists*. I was sure I wouldn't like it.

So I decided to live there.

It was the Foreign Affairs Office of the Shanghai Municipal People's Government that suggested it. I had established a nonprofit to encourage entrepreneurism in Singapore, and the people at the Foreign Affairs Office in Shanghai had the jolly idea that I could do the same there.

My reaction was to say, "Haven't you noticed all your tall buildings?" Did Shanghai really need my ideas to boost entrepreneurship?

The answer from the Foreign Affairs people surprised me. "Those are government-linked companies and foreign investors. We need local entrepreneurs. They don't need you in Guangzhou where everyone is an entrepreneur, but we need you here."

What I had experienced in Singapore for seven years was "China Light," that is, China with many Japanese characteristics. They spoke English, they waited in line, they didn't spit, they didn't buy gum. Shanghai would be a whole new adventure. I started with long visits, and then in early 2009 I moved to Shanghai and began renting a serviced apartment in the former French Concession. The basics were all taken care of by the ladies at the front desk. They could set up your phone, reserve a cab, or tell you where to shop for groceries and how to accomplish all the little tasks of daily living. It was a good first dip into living here but not the real thing; so after about a year I moved into my own apartment in the far more gritty Jing'An area. I was on my own. Sort of.

Life here is varied, interesting, colorful, and bombastic. The rich and the poor are cheek by jowl. Nanjing Road, one of the most fashionable, up-to-date streets in Shanghai, is only two blocks from where I live. All the big names, the ones known worldwide—Gucci, Armani, Hermes, Louis Vuitton—have shops here. US brands GAP, Levi's, American Eagle, Apple, Japanese Uniqlo, plus all the fine watch and electronic companies and many others as well, including local Shanghainese selling locally designed Chinese fashions, are arrayed along this street. Sorry, no Shanghai Tang.

The girls are glamorous and the tourists in knots. Step a block or two off Nanjing Xi Lu (once more alluringly called Bubbling Well Road) and behold: the driver of a Mercedes honking as he passes a pushcart man with his higgledy-piggledy pile of items for sale, items that somehow materialize into a small living. There are completely silent electric bikes next to rattling VWs, loud motorbikes next to smooth Bentleys and of course, bicycle riders and pedestrians in the midst of all this hodgepodge.

On a side street walking along the sidewalk your stride might be interrupted by an oblivious gentleman lying on his chaise lounge straddling the narrow sidewalk, newspaper held up and open in front of him. If you are tall, your head might be grazed by someone's drying laundry with all types of intimate items dangling above like some colorful awning. Grannies carry toddlers whose pants are split for easy crapping although rarely do they do it right in the street. A stray fruit seller may park curbside selling mangoes or chestnuts from the back of a rusting black bike. A man and his wife with a portable hot plate will be patting a hot, flat biscuit into shape, a snack made as you wait. Students with their red scarves pass to and from school looking for a sweet from peripatetic vendors who know their schedule as well as they do.

Living in a Communist country is not always what you expect. Once I went with my good friend Tom Klitgaard as he was receiving the Magnolia Award for service to Shanghai. He has steadfastly worked on the San Francisco–Shanghai Sister City organization for decades. We were picked up by a government official and driven to the guarded compound, which resembles a large park (only a tiny part of which we saw). We were brought to a two-story building and entered the vestibule where silk-clad young women in form-fitting *qi paos* greeted us as Tom registered and received his instructions for the award ceremony.

The building interior was one marble hall followed by another. It was opulence incarnate, with walls adorned by magnificent paintings at least six or seven feet tall. The room for the ceremony was spacious, and guests like me were placed in one part and those to receive the honors in another. There were at least ten officials in attendance. After a brief overall congratulatory speech each awardee was introduced and presented with a medal and certificate followed by a lavish buffet reception. My overall impression was "These are Communists?" Honestly everything about the ceremony, from the setting to the reception, rivaled anything the most extravagant nation might present.

Someone once told me a story set during Mao's reign. My friend was having dinner with a high official in Zhongnanhai,[1] the very private area next to the Forbidden City that houses the top Party offices and government officials. The official was wearing his Mao jacket and drab clothing. But the evening was hot; as it got warmer the official unbuttoned his uniform-like jacket, and slightly exposed was a beautiful silk shirt. He could see my friend was surprised.

"We keep the beauty on the inside, not the outside," the official said.

As I've discovered in my years in China, this is less and less true.

I see the order and disorder all at once, modern and ancient, rich and super rich mingling with those who just get along. Here is life in your face. My own reactions surprise me. I'm not put off by the complexity and lack of Western harmony that tends to segregate by neighborhood and many other ways. It's okay to live life out in the open, even as the country gallops along toward whatever is to come.

---

[1]. It is often used as a metonym for the Chinese leadership at large (in the same sense that the term White House frequently refers to the President of the United States and his associates). The most important entrance to the compound is the southern one at Xinhuamen (Xinhua Gate, or "Gate of New China"), surrounded by two slogans: "long live the great Communist Party of China" and "long live the invincible Mao Zedong Thought." The view behind the entrance is shielded by a traditional screen wall with the slogan "Serve the People," written in the handwriting of Mao Zedong.

# Chapter 2

## *Getting to Know You*

China has the same landmass as the United States, with about 1 billion more people. Shanghai has twenty-three million of which about 125,000 are foreigners and 27,000, or 0.1 percent, are American. The Han people have inhabited and ruled China for most of its long history. There are fifty-five minority groups. The big exceptions to Han dominance are fierce riders from the north, Mongolian Genghis Khan, and the Qing Manchus, finally exhausted and defunct in 1912.

To try to get a feel for this country's long history you need to know there have been only six ruling dynasties since the fall of the Roman Empire. There has been almost uninterrupted trade with the rest of the world, both through the Silk Roads and from the sea. About ninety years before Columbus, in 1405 the Ming Emperor Yongle sent out his sea captain Zheng He, who voyaged with huge ships throughout Southeast Asia, Africa, and the Middle East. China didn't seek to conquer. They gathered information, unique things, and sometimes sought suzerainty. The next emperor burned the ships—he had dozens of motivations, but the venture cost too much and it was time to turn inward. Between strong dynasties, warlords (who dominated their own fiefdoms) were constantly pulling apart vast regions of the country until they were brought into the fold. Mao was the last consolidator and stability remains the most important government and party consideration. All wisdom of China flows from understanding this.

China is surrounded by fifteen countries, and some of them not too friendly. Japan, Russia, India, and Vietnam, just in our memory have all had fights with China, or China picked fights with them. Americans would likely have a different outlook on national security if instead of two benign neighbors we had Russia, Japan, Iran, Kazakhstan, North Korea, Pakistan, and a few others next door who didn't care for us much. Furthermore what if in the ebb and flow of forming the country Tibet, Xinjiang Uyghur Autonomous Region, what Islamist secessionists call

East Turkistan, and the Inner Mongolia Autonomous Region were lopped off? About one third or more of China would disappear. Goodbye Texas, New Mexico, Arizona, Alaska, and the Louisiana Purchase.

Being a large landmass with diverse peoples makes you realize you can't think of a uniform China. The north eats noodles, the south rice. Somewhere just above Shanghai and the Yangtze River, or the Qin Mountains and Huai River, divides the two areas. Then there is out west with the Uyghurs and Tibetans. Floating off the coast, the pesky Taiwanese. In between are geographic pockets of ethnicity, economic disparity, and clans. Think of Xi Jinping, the president, driving a Roman chariot with the galloping horses representing the twenty-three provinces, five autonomous regions, two special administrative regions, and four municipalities. Giddyup to the twenty-first century. At the same time he must continue the nearly forty-year transformation taking the average citizen from utter poverty to modern life. When Mao died, the country changed horses in midstream. It's almost as if America went from the eighteenth century to the twenty-first, skipping over all the intervening steps of acclimating the secure knowledge and institutions for each new step. This is the New China, but you can still cross a street and dodge down an alley and be back in old China. Mao was right when he proclaimed "China has stood up," but it is not quite straight yet.

It also helps to understand China to consider if the United States had a treaty that had been made with a powerful country, say England, to have absolute sovereignty in part of New York City. They get to control Manhattan. When France hears about this they decide to dominate Brooklyn, and a handful of countries take over Staten Island leaving the Bronx and Queens for the local authorities to administer. Oh yes, by the way, you couldn't go to Manhattan or any of the other "concessions" unless the British or other countries let you. Part of the concession was that throughout the nation you had to allow the importation and sale of dope. This was Shanghai, and China, from the 1840s to the 1940s. And imagine that the most productive part of the country for almost fifteen years was forcibly occupied and administered by the hated Japanese.

So as we grapple with trying to understand China of today we need to be less dogmatic and more understanding of what ingredients go into its thinking as China finds its way into the community of nations.

❧ ❧ ❧

My first trip to China in 1986 was part of a brief journey I organized for myself to introduce me to Asia. I went to Japan, China, Singapore, and on to Australia and New Zealand, which I thought were "right there" tucked in next to the rest of Southeast Asia. My ignorance of the region was unbounded.

I had long worked in the merger and acquisition field. My company was founded in 1971 and originally based in San Francisco. We focused primarily in the merger and acquisition field with its specialty in insurance-related companies. We gradually added offices in New York and Texas and partners in London and Tokyo. Only later after many trips to Asia did we establish a headquarters in Singapore. When we established an Asian investment fund I hoped to invest in Tian'an Insurance in Shanghai. At the time the Chinese financial regulations precluded our efforts. Tian'an Insurance, which was then a very small company, today has become a huge business worth billions.

I flew United Airlines to Beijing just months after they had acquired the routes from failing Pan Am. It was my first trip to China, and I remember distinctly that it mildly annoyed me that none of the announcements were in Chinese. How would Americans feel coming into Washington, DC, on a foreign airliner and have no English announcements? I think this must have been because the United crews were new to the route and hadn't yet sorted out bilingual personnel.

The man sitting next to me sold shoes and was coming home from a business trip in New Jersey. This was very early days, and as I think of it now he was a pioneer in a country that eventually became the largest source of shoes in the world. When I was in business the shoes in my closet were all British, Alan McAfee leather. That's because when I was in my twenties my dad bought me a pair like he had and I continued to buy the same sorts of shoes throughout my working career. Two brown, two black. Identical plain style. McAfee has since ceased making shoes and now my closet is an eclectic mix of what we used to call "tennis shoes" and a few dress pairs. Those old McAfees are still good. Regardless of brand, I have no doubt every other shoe in my closet was manufactured in China.

The Beijing airport had corrugated roofing. It had no planes, no cars, no passengers, not a single shop. Walking out, you went through swinging double-doors with thick rubber strips as they joined, making it a push to get out. Outside there were a few taxis parked right at the entrance. My taxi was dirty and old and the driver was young and reckless. The road from the airport was two lanes and unlit.

The first night I ever spent in China, this land where I have now spent over five fascinating years, was at the Sheraton Great Wall Hotel, which the government had built in 1984 and was at that time either the only or one of the very few Western hotels. By 1986 the room walls were already cracked and peeling, but everything else was pretty standard hotel fare. Nothing fancy but adequate.

Bob Theleen told me a story of the same hotel where he came with another foreigner and they went into the bar in the evening. There was a dance band but of course no one to dance with. His friend took it upon himself to complain to the manager. How could they attract guests to a bar and not have some females in attendance for dancing? Honest to God, about twenty minutes later in marched a small contingent of the People's Liberation Army female soldiers, in uniform, and the first soldier approached Bob and said, "I am Miss Li of the People's Liberation Army; will you dance with me?"

From my room I could look down the very wide North Dong San Huan Road, just over the treetops. Early in the morning I looked out and I couldn't quite tell what I was seeing since it was still dark. Finally I realized I was seeing the heads of thousands of black-haired bicycle riders flowing in an unending stream down the avenue. It was mesmerizing. I have never seen anything like it before or since.

In those days there literally were no private cars, and only occasionally would you see an army truck slowly navigating the sea of bicycles. Cabs were so rare that you had to book one early in the morning and keep it through the night because you would never be able to get another. One day, looking out the taxi's windshield, the sea of bicycles would part just inches before we very slowly overtook them, as if the people could see behind them and moved at just the perfect instant to avoid a collision. We were like scuba divers, languidly swimming though a school of fish. An all-day booking might have cost all of US $5; the image of the "parting seas" remains with me today.

Naturally, I visited all the normal tourist sites, including waxen Mao. Mao dead was not so formidable, somewhat rumpled and not entirely deferred to by the guard who kept you moving, as if there wasn't that much worth seeing here. There was a sign that said "Take off your hat and keep your mouth shut." That sort of sums it up.

I went to the Beijing Opera, the theater nearly as sparse as the airport. People today would find that hard to believe with the opulence of newly built venues in Beijing and Shanghai. The seats were more like benches—no velvet cushions there—and the Chinese characters shown on vertical screens on either side of the stage seemed to be operated by hand slides. I asked some Europeans why there had to be these characters shown as the action proceeded and was told that often it was hard to understand what was being said along with the fact that some Chinese words have multiple meanings, so the characters clarify the action. This is true in Japan as well, where you often see people in conversation making kanji on their palms to explain meaning.

The Friendship store was the only place a foreigner could buy anything, and I took the advice of a friend and picked up silk pajamas for what I assumed, or hoped, was a very inexpensive price (having never bought silk pajamas I was also ignorant what they would cost anywhere else). I also bought a few Tang-era horse reproductions, which I doubted would ever make it home unbroken, but somehow, packed in a huge wooden crate, they did and still sit in my living room in my home in San Francisco. During a party I subsequently had at home I saw the director of the Asian Art Museum carefully look at them, no doubt concluding they were what they were but being too polite to comment.

What I really wanted to see in Beijing were the inside of the *hutongs*, where most people lived at that time. Today they are almost nonexistent although efforts are now being made to preserve what remains. I don't know if it was forbidden, but in general foreigners were pretty much kept to the main tourist sites and so was I. The only times I've seen the inside courtyards and the interiors of the buildings have been in Chinese movies.

Something we could learn from China are the descriptive and exotic names given to gates, gardens, and just quiet spots. The Spot of Return for Reading. What a glorious name. The Garden of Harmonious Interest or the Gates of Luminous Virtue and Correct Conduct. The halls of Diligence, Discernment, Honesty, and Open-Mindedness. Gardens and pavilion names are the best. The Garden of the Humble Administrator (who by the extravagance of the garden wasn't so humble), Pavilion in the Lotus Breeze, Listening to the Rain Pavilion, Watching the Pines and Appreciating Paintings Hall, the Lingering Garden; these latter in Suzhou.

When I first visited it was winter and periodically you would see a big pyramid of cabbages that had been dumped on a street corner by a truck. These were for people to take home. Then those cabbages would make the journey up into apartments and reappear in the winter air, propped on the little railings outside apartment windows; there weren't many refrigerators in Chinese homes then so keeping food in the cool air was just as good.

As I left Beijing for the first time I had to fight my way through a scrum of people all thrusting their reservations in the face of one stoic clerk. It was every man for himself. This turned out to be the modus operandi anywhere you would normally queue. I got smart my second trip to China and hired the Communist Party travel agency to guide me. No more scrums. The guy would march to the front of the chaos, flip out his credentials and immediately be taken care of. My boarding pass in hand, we would march to the gate and be first in line.

That has its advantages and its disadvantages. I remember feeling very guilty when a guide and I approached the frontier from China to Hong Kong. In those days Hong Kong was still a foreign country so the frontier was a hell of a mess. Hundreds of people trying to get to the immigration officers. Not I; head of the line amid death stares. The guide flips out his CCP credentials. Stamp, stamp, and off I go through the barriers, faintly hearing the twanging sound of bowstrings unleashing a thousand angry arrows flying at my back.

# Chapter 3

## *What Brought Me to China*

We started Spirit of Enterprise China in January 2008, twenty-two years after that first visit to China. The Foreign Affairs Office of the Shanghai government suggested that it would be a good idea to bring the concept we'd used in Singapore to it. That struck me initially as a bit bizarre since there was so much business activity going on already, but I was cautioned that it was not their local entrepreneurs who were doing it; rather it was government-linked companies and foreign investors.

So I started. Initially I managed with frequent visits and emails, but soon realized I needed to be there more, which pushed me to get an apartment and stay in Shanghai at least while things got settled in. It was an optimist's outlook, probably similar to many first-time investors in China, which didn't quite work out as planned. We had to build it from scratch.

But in order to explain Spirit of Enterprise China I have to engage in a little history about Spirit of Enterprise Singapore. More than ten years ago, I was inspired while listening to the Singapore prime minister's annual National Day Rally speech. Prime Minister Goh Chock Tong suggested that Singapore didn't have enough of the "the spirit of enterprise." I had just wound up my last fund, Ascendant Capital Partners, and was looking for something productive to do. When I heard the speech I thought that it was absurd that Singapore entrepreneurs existed but were not recognized by the government, as they should be. The government was claiming that there were no entrepreneurs in their society.

I believed that was not true. In the Singapore government's mind at the time, an entrepreneur was Bill Gates or some of the big local entrepreneurs. My idea was to help people recognize the existence of more humble entrepreneurs and the value of their work. I even found some data that showed small businesses were the backbone of any economy and the major job creator. Just to show them that they needed to change their view I started Spirit of Enterprise, initially with no backing and no employees.

Shortly after the National Day speech, while walking through Raffles Place, a square in the heart of Singapore's business area, I noticed a cobbler and his assistant working on the sidewalk next to one of the city's tallest skyscrapers, Republic Plaza. I thought, "He's an entrepreneur." Then I saw a money changer's kiosk briskly doing business and close by a chicken-rice stand and then a person selling sweets from their small glass cabinet. All of them were entrepreneurs in my mind. They just weren't recognized by the government as entrepreneurs; only the flashy, big electronics companies or developers were entrepreneurs that counted in the mind of the government. I decided to change that perception and show that even someone with a self-manned food stand should be considered an entrepreneur and receive as much honour (as they spell it), admiration, and public recognition as the "bigwigs."

Initially I thought of it as a book with photos highlighting these unseen lives, but after a visit with a good friend, Tan Kin Lian, who at the time was the CEO of the largest local insurance company, NTUC Income, I changed my perspective. Kin Lian suggested we get students to interview entrepreneurs and put the stories on the web. He turned over his special assistant for charitable efforts, plus his public relations and design team, plus his mailing list, and most importantly, gave his energy and creativity to get started.

I reached in and backed the now-developing idea with a little stipend and hired two part-time ladies to begin to address administrative tasks. Ms. Kelly Teoh was the first hire and she wonderfully saw us through almost all of the first decade. In 2002 I don't think we even had the money to pay her enough to buy her lunches but she was inspired and inspirational and well connected to groups I was not, plus she always had a contagious smile. A lot of the success that was yet a glimmer and an idea was transformed by her practicality, hard work, and organization.

In the inaugural press conference announcing Spirit of Enterprise Singapore we used a worker's singlet to represent honest, hard-working people creating businesses.

Many told me it was a futile idea and that the government would never pay any attention anyway. The long and short of it can be seen on the Singapore website (www.soe.org.sg) and the award-ceremony page (spiritofenterprise.us/awards&honorees). Yes, the program developed into 152 nominated entrepreneurs interviewed by students from the top universities and through a public, online voting system, thirty-eight honorees were chosen to receive the Spirit of Enterprise Award. We chose thirty-eight (another Kin Lian idea) in keeping with the fact that it was the thirty-eighth year of Singapore becoming a nation. I am pleased to say that the Singapore government and people did pay attention; the President of Singapore, S. R. Nathan, presented the awards at our third ceremony.

But I think my proudest personal moment came at the first awards ceremony, which we held outside the Asian Civilisations Museum. I stood at one end of a footbridge with Minister of State Raymond Lim Siang Keat and Tan Kin Lian, greeting the first honorees who marched behind a formed unit of the National Defense Forces marching band, all spiffed up in their dress whites. Standing at the opposite end of the Cavenagh Bridge you can readily see its sloping apex. First the band music came floating above the Singapore River, and very gradually you could see the top of those white hats and finally the whole marching band, in stunning formation and headed straight toward us to begin the first Spirit of Enterprise awards.

As part of the program the student interviews were turned into a book and distributed free to the universities and sold in bookstores. In subsequent years there have been thirteen books published. Ten in Singapore, two in China in Chinese, one in Mauritius, and one set of interviews online in Vietnam. To view a sample of the books take a look at www.spiritofenterprise.us

The Singapore experience provided many wonderful moments, especially my interaction with the entrepreneurs. I remember so well a married couple who ran a small Chinese medicine shop in a open-area series of counter shops. Here's how it originally appeared in the SOE interview by Veronica Tan Hui Min from Nanyang Technological University.

*Tucked into a narrow five-foot way alcove behind a line of shady trees, the forty-six-year-old Chinese medical hall is not immediately visible from the hustle and bustle of the ever-busy Queen Street, thronged by devout Buddhists who pay tribute at the century old Kwan Yin Temple just fifty paces away. Moreover, the shop is rendered more unobtrusive due to the fact that it is located smack in the middle of a row of no less than six medical halls with another three just across the street. Yet the simply furnished shop commands a charm that contin-*

ues to draw in a string of customers during the entire time I was there.

And that remarkable coziness one feels upon entering lends itself from Hog Seng's two young proprietors, Darrel and Elizabeth Mok, both still in their thirties and married to each other with three children. The couple is delightful. Both are warm and friendly, greeting customers promptly as they enter the store and eager to attend to your needs. One feels immediately at peace in the air suffused with the bittersweet scent of pao shen and the soft lilt of Christian music playing in the background. Not quite your average Chinese medical hall, which leaves the unwitting patron to fend for himself among shelves upon shelves of strange concoctions and where a purchase is merely deemed transactional.

They sat behind their glass display case and made their living. They told this story.

"Last year, there was a couple that came to my shop who had an eleven-year-old boy who had asthma since he was a child. What happened was that the doctors wanted to increase his dosage of the steroids to control his condition. However the parents were not very open to that because they were afraid that they would have to keep increasing the dosage. So out of desperation, I would say, they were recommended by our close friends to our shop and we actually prescribed the medicine to him made of pure Chinese herbs, which is a prescription from my father. And I used the prescription to give to this couple to their little boy and within two days of taking that medication the boy was having relief from his asthma. This dear couple has since become our friends."

Elizabeth says of her aspiration, "I feel that dollars-and-cents is a very myopic and short-term goal, because it is not going to bring you very far as I feel that our career and our business is going to be lifelong. It is a marathon, not just a hundred-meter sprint. And I feel that if the goal is measured in dollars and cents, when you get there the satisfaction drops and ends there, you see. Many a time the hearts of my husband and I are warmed not by good sales figures but instances like that testimony I was sharing with you about that eleven-year-old boy. These are things that will stay with you forever.'"

What a wonderful outlook. What a wonderful couple.

One more intrepid entrepreneur tells what happens when you don't do things right. Eddie Gan Eng Hui, also of Nanyang, tells the story. I've shortened it a bit.

Meet Dave Yiu, one of Singapore's very own self-made entrepreneurs. His business is scuba diving, the sport once considered by many to be hazardous and something only the brave hearts will try.

Dave says, "We went through a lot in the sense that I wanted to be a little bit different from the rest. We wanted a place of our own. We started off running all our trips to Malaysia. We build a small resort on Pulau Aur.... Financing was hard to get.... In the early days, it was difficult especially for a brand new company to be set up and no collateral to get a loan to try to make it big. It was very tough.

We faced a lot of problems particularly because our diving activities were seasonal. You can't really scuba dive in Singapore. The best place is in Malaysia. That's where we have part of our roots and come monsoon times, we suffered very heavy blows financially to keep the company afloat. We have one of the first few proper dive boats around.... We didn't quite design it properly and sad to say, that boat sank. Fortunately there was nobody on board except our crew. That took the company down a bit, a few rungs down the ladder we were climbing. That costs us a fortune in terms of our reputation because once we had some small mishaps, although nobody was injured at all because we did not have any divers onboard, but that cost us quite a lot of money to recover the boat, not to mention the cost of refurbishing it.

That was the maiden voyage, actually a trial run to the island. And it sank. Weeks were spent locating it because it sank in the night and we were fortunate it sank near an island. That was a big shock to me. At that point of time, I was on the island when the phone call came twelve hours after it sank. We were already making plans to look for the boat. It was very normal for boats to go missing during the early days when you have a lot of Kalimantan haze; the fog and navigating to the island wasn't easy especially we always travel at night and that being a maiden voyage, it really got me worried. We spent a couple of weeks looking for our sunken boat and a lot of money went out. That was near the start of the season. We spent so much money to do the boat and it sank.

You needed basic marine engineering; I have to talk to friends and come up with drawings. Things back then were done the 'kampong' way. You saw a picture on the magazine. You want your boat to look like that. You give it to a carpenter and he will just do it. He did not have any marine engineering experience. That was one of the reasons why the boat went down. We were very fortunate there was nobody onboard, no injuries although the boat went down. No accidents involving any person except our crew who were all swimmers because they are all seagoing people. They managed to swim to a nearby island within the hour although it was in the middle of the night. That was one of the worst times I can remember.

I started as a kid, fishing out at sea, spending my whole holidays out at sea, which incidentally is how I came about doing this because of my love for the sea, *and the days I gone out fishing and the many close calls I had with life and death, with boats, ships, and motors. I started going out to sea at the age of eight. I pretty much live an adventurous life."*²

To call this simply an adventurous life.... Can you imagine? But Dave persisted and never gave up. He now has several resorts and many seaworthy, well-designed boats. I just love his story; it really epitomizes in my mind the difficulty of becoming an entrepreneur and the "never give up" attitude of them all.

Often I'm asked about the qualities of entrepreneurs. You can get the sense of what's in the books from those two stories. One inspiring story after another; tragedy, comedy, near-death experiences, market collapse, rows between partners, everything. But there is one recurrent theme though all the stories, all the books, and that is never give up. No matter what befell these single-minded women and men they would never let themselves give up.

I am especially fond of that first group of awardees in 2003. What a thrill to see them and get to know them. In subsequent years many have accomplished well beyond what anyone could have thought when they were marching across the Cavenagh Bridge. Some of that inaugural class are:

Charles Wong Mun Hwa, who with his brother started a business selling very inexpensive women's shoes. Charles & Keith is now in multiple lines of women's goods, is in forty companies and has a large expansion effort going on in China.

Steven Fang, who has built Cordlife from a small local business to an international biotech company.

Adrin Loi Boon Sim, who took his grandfather's coffee "joint" and made it into the household franchise of Ya Kun Kaya Toast. They are just opening their first outlet in Shanghai.

Dr. Rosemary Tan Sok Pin of Genecet Biotechnologies, a brilliant scientist who has developed, among other things, kits that identify multiple viruses in very quick time. She was the first to figure out a test for SARS—severe acute respiratory syndrome—that hit so devastatingly (and thankfully, briefly) in late 2002.

Eddie Chau of e-Cop.net, who created a masterful company to track down and prevent viruses from attacking your computers. His early office looked like a war room, highlighting in real time the attacks of virus perpetrators.

Don Lim, who started as a cook in the Hewlett Packard cafeteria. He decided to go off on his own to be the creator of the best chicken pies in Southeast Asia: Don Your Personal Pie Club.

And finally my friend Viswa Sadasivan, who created The Right Angle Group (now, Strategic Moves) to produce and create media and went on to be named to parliament by the Singapore government. These are just a few of the more than 1,500 that have now been profiled by the Spirit of Enterprise.

From my many efforts at encouraging entrepreneurism I've often talked about the difference in making a living and making a business. Normally just making a living doesn't often create additional jobs except for a limited number of family members, while even the smallest business tends to hire new people as it grows.

A good illustration of the effect of a small business is the story of three Singaporeans who were among the first honorees of the Spirit of Enterprise. All three worked in Silicon Valley in California for a software company, and they dreamed of creating their own tech company when they moved back to Singapore. Very often these young men would meet at a local shop, talk, and drink smoothies.

One day one of them held up the drink and said, "You know these are really good; I wonder if it would be a good business in Singapore." Out went the dream of tech and in came the dream of soft drinks. They subsequently bought the franchise for Southeast Asia and today they have more than twenty outlets in Singapore and multiple ancillary businesses.

What I really like about the story is this; in each shop it takes about five people to run it. Three of the people have to be well trained and are normally quite young. The other two do the cleanup and other tasks and are usually elderly people. Often they are retirees or had been made redundant by high-tech companies—they otherwise couldn't get a job. So you have two groups, the youth and the elderly, one hundred people who are making incomes. If the founding three young men had gone into tech probably these kinds of people would never have gotten jobs.

Many times after a lecture at a university or just talking to young people about starting their own business I encourage them to look at sectors that are demeaned by the smart-ass MBAs as they flock to consulting firms or Wall Street. I tell them to get into businesses that others eschew. Or, why not try some businesses that not many people are in because they are not prestigious or "clean"? Sometimes businesses that were started by first-generation family members seem too mean for the university or MBA graduate. They feel funny about the fact their father may be in the laundry business, or reconstituted oil, or farming. My view is this is just the kind of business that often has little sophisticated competition and often has not upgraded for technology or modern techniques and could be enhanced by the next generation. I'm afraid some of the students are carried away by the glitter of tech and the chimera of fast money.

When I was finishing my book on entrepreneurism in Singapore my editor eschewed the fact that the final quote was from a goat farmer and hence in her National University of Singapore background was not very worthy of quoting. "Who listens to goat farmers?" That's the kind of mindset that I would love youthful entrepreneurs to compete against.

One final note on Singapore entrepreneurs. Kho Ah Hee was a cobbler on Malacca Street at the foot of Republic Plaza office tower. He sat on the curb with his small box of tools and one assistant and fixed shoes all day. He is the person I first noticed when I was thinking about "invisible" entrepreneurs. Purposefully I had our student interviews do him as the inaugural interview. Our first students, who were from National University of Singapore, Choy Kein Wai and Mabel Yeo Koh Sing, did it in Cantonese, the only language Kho was fluent in. He told a simple story of perseverance and self-reliance. He had put two kids though university, paid his taxes, had a steady living, and was highly regarded around Raffles Place.

To everyone's surprise Kho's interview struck a real chord with those who read it online, and it garnered enough votes on the SOE internet voting to put him on the list of awardees for the first awards ceremony. Sadly he had a stroke prior to the event and hence could not attend. He remains an inspiration at least to me, but I would guess many.

During the interview he was asked whom he admired and he said the owner of Republic Plaza, Singapore billionaire Kwek Leng Beng. Sometime after, while chatting about the cobbler to Leng Beng I told him how the cobbler admired him. He said, "I don't know him." I retorted by asking him if he knew the only difference between them. He was stumped. "The only difference between you two is that you have more money!" I told him. He laughed and said I was right. Later he ordered multiple copies of our book to give to all who came to his office as inspiration to the long line of those seeking funds from him to start their businesses. He became a very generous donor to SOE. One time I ran into him at Changi Airport and asked him what he was doing there?

"Why don't you have a private plane?" I asked.

"Because all my friends do."

Very funny, and the sign of someone who knows not only how to make a buck, but keep it.

I found Singapore to be a totally free city-state except you can't mess in politics if you are a foreigner. You can't even give a political donation, which I discovered when I tried to do so for one of my friends, a member of parliament and minister. For Singaporeans you can form political parties and you can run candidates for election. There are many hurdles the ruling PAP (People's Action Party) puts in front of you, but at the end of the day it is a functioning democracy with heavy-handed management from the top. This began in the early days in 1965 after the British left their former colony and Malaysia had kicked them out. There was no certainty about how things would turn out and a strong Communist Party was trying to become the ruling coalition. Lee Kuan Yew, the George Washington of Singapore, is quoted as saying, "I carry my own hatchet." He used it to crush the opposition and set up one of the most prosperous countries in the world. When Deng Xiaoping took over China he came calling for advice. Years later a story circulated that when Lee Kuan Yew was in China he had publicly mentioned many improvements that he thought should be made. When these were reported to Deng, he apocryphally said, "I greatly admire Prime Minister Lee, and if he lived here I would give him a small city to run."

There is a place in Singapore called Speaker's Corner, which was established to let people share their views and vent their opinions. But not foreigners. And those who are allowed to speak have multiple can'ts and musts. They can't deal with religious subjects or "or any subject which may cause feelings of enmity, hatred, ill-will, or hostility between different racial or religious groups." They also can't speak without registering, can't use a high-powered microphone; must sign up in advance at the attached police station if they intend to speak; and must speak only in the official four languages or related dialects of Singapore. None of these rules are particularly onerous or even unreasonable, but it is not exactly like the speaker's corner in London. I lived quite close to Speaker's Corner and not once in seven years did I see anyone speaking there. The atmosphere such rules create may explain why so many people believe that the government listens in on phone conversations, especially foreigners' phone calls (what a boring job if it really exists).

In a conversation with a minister, Vivian Balakrishnan, I said, "Oh my, if you don't like what I'm doing, poor me, you might deport me to the United States." Just like Br'er Rabbit not wanting to be thrown into the briar patch. We both had a good laugh but unfortunately for native Singaporeans, challenging the government isn't often pleasant. It is curious—senior government officials are in the main really talented and dedicated people, the crème de la crème of public servants. But they have this overarching belief that what they are doing is the way it needs to be done and are very resistant to outside input. This may be because they probably have thoroughly researched and vetted the subject and hence feel that they have looked at all reasonable angles. Especially with the "top of the heap" ministers, there is more than a taint of arrogance. This is not true of all of them (certainly Minister Balakrishnan wasn't like that but then, he is an ethnic Indian in a Chinese cabinet).

The most egregious example of arrogance I saw from a minister was a verbal dispute that arose during a friendly luncheon with about ten others. He proclaimed that the United States didn't allow dual citizenship. I told him that indeed it did, but he wouldn't hear of it. Later I went back to my office, pulled up the official US State Department site that clearly stated that the United States does allow dual citizenship. I sent it to him with a polite note. His response was along the lines of "no, but," trying to justify his incorrect perspective. He just wouldn't accept being wrong. Another example was when I was asked to help the now president, Tony Tan, draft a speech encouraging entrepreneurism. I said, tell them to "challenge authority." He looked at me like W. C. Fields in that famous photo of him slyly looking over his poker hand. I'm sure he was thinking, "How did this guy get in the room?"

The government is super sensitive regarding religious and racial matters that may cause disharmony. In 1964 there were two race riots between Chinese and Malay Singaporeans. This energized the leadership who then and there decided no such thing would ever happen again. It could ruin Singapore, a small city surrounded by two large neighbors, Malaysia and Indonesia. This was the year before Singapore was thrown out of the Federation of Malaysia, partially in fear of the Chinese population causing an overthrow of the Malaysian political elite. They were afraid of the effectiveness of the Chinese-dominated People's Action Party as a political force. Unfortunately, in less than four years riots broke out in Malaysia against Chinese Malaysians. As my Chinese driver in Kuala Lumpur years later told me: "I carry two passports." I asked why and he answered, "Sometimes they kill us." Today both countries are very careful about protecting their ethnic dominance.

Singapore is always alert and sensitive to its size and vulnerability. The whole community was really annoyed when the President of Indonesia pejoratively called it a "little red dot" on the map. Funny enough this insult has become a sense of pride with Singaporeans.[3]

One of the things that made my time in Singapore so successful was that the government, once they spot you and figure out you have something to offer, seeks you out to make a better country by inviting you on various boards and committees aimed at improving some aspect of the country.

They actually listen to the recommendations of these boards. For example I was on a board whose sole task was to seek out old business and finance laws that not only no longer served their intended purpose but now obstructed commerce. We identified many, and lo and behold they reviewed them and then sent our recommendations to parliament, which did away with them. They also listened to ideas that they had resisted in the past. We suggested an over-the-counter stock market, which traditionally in various countries is the first step for a growing company to get capital. This is inherently risky because many of these companies are quite small and often don't do well over the long term. Singapore is risk-averse for its citizens, especially using their spare investment funds. Over-the-counter markets are often referred to as "curb" markets because they start with buyers and sellers outside on the street gathered together. This is exactly how the New York Stock Exchange is supposed to have evolved. We presented our case and it was accepted on a very small scale, with many limits, but indeed it was started.

I was on another board whose purpose was to invest in new company projects that had a high probability of failure. That's correct, a high probability of failure, but these projects were considered worth the try for the innovation they might bring. Board members would get a fat binder delivered to us a week or so prior to a meeting, prepared by our secretariat. It included the four or so companies that were going to present to us at the board meeting and also included all the proposals that were deemed not of sufficient quality to be considered. This second category provided the much-needed comic relief from reading through the reports. For example we had one man who proposed a new government program to eradicate dengue, which is a fever caused by mosquitoes. His proposal was voluminous, and the final page revealed that he had modified a fly swatter. We passed on it.

I was living in Singapore when the first plane hit the World Trade Center. I got a call from Ann Miller in the United States who said, "I think a private plane just crashed into the World Trade Center; turn on your TV." By the time I did, the second plane had hit, and we all knew this was something different. It was night in Singapore. It was 9/11.

Being far away from home made me feel closer to my country than one normally does. It is events of unusual importance that elicit a feeling of belonging and patriotism. The next day, on the way to my office in Raffles Place, a TV crew spotted me and headed in my direction. I waved them off. They understood. Americans were in mourning. Give us a little time.

The government of Singapore responded magnificently. Not just the normal diplomatic statements but they organized a memorial service in the National Stadium a few evenings later. My expectation was that maybe a few thousand Americans would show up and maybe some of the government ministers. I had no expectations but wanted to go and share my grief and determination with those few who would participate. When I walked into the stadium I was dumbfounded. It was jammed, and not primarily Americans or Europeans but by Singaporeans. Just folks there to say they were sorry about what had happened to their friend, their ally, and ultimate protector. The entire government showed up, from Lee Kwan Yu, the prime minister, and the entire cabinet. The ceremony itself was a combination of multiple religious leaders offering prayers to the head of the American chamber of commerce offering a touching tribute to all those who perished. There were other short tributes and inspirations, but the most moving part of the ceremony—other than the crowd—was at the end candles were lit all over the stadium and everyone sang. I don't remember what the song was but it didn't matter; we were all together.

These were seven very good years. Spirit of Enterprise Singapore celebrated its eleventh anniversary in 2013.

**2**. Excerpt from *Singapore's Homegrown Entrepreneurs Tell You How to Do It*. (City: Landmark Books, 2003).

**3**. "Little red dot" is an epithet used to refer to Singapore in a disparaging manner by former Indonesian President B. J. Habibie. It has come to be used with pride and a sense of the nation's success despite its physical limitations.

# Chapter 4

## *Shanghai Life*

To "look through my eyes" and see Shanghai as I do, you must first understand that I grew up in a very small city compared to this one. When I was a child in San Francisco it was a small enough place that you went to kindergarten in the same school where your mother, uncles, and aunts had gone. My sister and brothers preceded and followed me there. The children you met there remained acquaintances, if not friends, for the rest of your life. You followed each other in your first dancing class at Mr. Kitchen's (a place you couldn't escape, no matter how much you begged your mother not to make you go). You went through your early life, through school, through this progression of dancing lessons and almost into college with many of the same neighborhood kids.

I remember playing in the street as a youngster and having my grandmother drive by. She'd stop and inspect me, then decide my T-shirt was not enough and tell me to put on a sweater. It was as if the city was a neighborhood. My grandfather, whom we called Pa, lived a few doors away in the house where my mother was born. I had aunts, uncles, and cousins living within walking distance. As an elementary-school student you could take the streetcar or "dinky" cable car (that's what we always called the Clay-Washington line to differentiate it from the much-larger California line) home from school without your mother worrying at all.

It was inevitable that wherever you went someone knew you or your family. Even the police (or cops as we called them) interacted with you. When I was in high school, a group of us decided it would be a grand idea to climb up inside one of the landmark buildings, the Palace of Fine Arts, which was left over from the 1915 Panama-Pacific Exposition. Noted Bay Area architect Bernard Maybeck had designed it in the Grecian style, with Corinthian columns, but it was just a shell, a structure with nothing inside it. It was at that time still made out of its original hardened papier-mâché so if you really tried—as we did—you could plop off big chunks in your hand.

We climbed to the very top and went outside the dome on a thin ledge and pushed a few of the faux Greek urns into the duck pond about ten stories below. There were big splashes and ducks flying, and then, at the exit, a squad car of San Francisco's finest waiting for us. Oh no! There we were, wearing our telltale St. Ignatius jackets and caught red handed. What did the cops do? They took our names and said if they ever caught us again they would call our mothers.

Our doors were always unlocked. The ice man came up from the basement and slid his ice into the top half of the ice box. The delivery boy came up the back stairs and left the groceries on the kitchen table. George came on Fridays and set new wood and coal in the fireplaces and did the heavy cleaning, like washing the front steps. He always sat in his yellow Mercury, parked at the corner and ate lunch by himself. A young black man named Buchanan washed the windows periodically. The names float up through time to me, making up the panoply of life growing up. There were Jack and Lee, Claude and Marie, Van, Mrs. Rutledge the baby nurse, and Dr. Gelston the family doctor with his Parker 51 pen and handy, long "needle" to lance our earaches as he sat at our bedside. Lois, a former movie actress turned governess, later a Yellow Cab driver. Mary, the Japanese day cleaner. We knew the grocery man, the butcher (Herman), the laundry man (Mr. Bedacaré). Then there was Emma, who cooked for us and "whooped" us if we were bad. She came from the Deep South. Her slave father had been freed by Abraham Lincoln's Emancipation Proclamation, or as Emma called it, so aptly, "the day freedom cried out." We learned the smell of collard greens, black-eyed peas, and the most wonderful cornbread in the world from her. She carried a straight razor in her purse and said, "no one is going to mess with you kids." We periodically begged her to show us the straight razor in her purse, the same way we would ask to be shown the gun of the beat cop who came by to collect a monthly fee for special watching of the neighborhood. "No one is going to mess with you kids," she said. San Francisco was a town in which Emma could buy a house for her large family not ten blocks from ours. Our families knew each other. Her son, whom we all called Sonny Boy, would come in by the back and sometimes sit in the kitchen. Emma started with our family in the forties and died with us in the sixties, and in some small ways, we remained intertwined. When my mother died in 1987 I noticed a black man I didn't know at her funeral. It was Sonny Boy, who had read her obituary in the paper and come to pay his respects.

Within such a community, you never knew when someone from the past might resurface and even come to your aid. Once I was down at the docks giving a speech as a candidate for congress to the laborers' union, one of the roughest, toughest bunch of men in the city. Internally, I was quaking in my boots. The audience looked at me like a kid and didn't react at all to my best lines. I finished to modest, intermittent applause. As I stood dumbly on the stage, out of the corner of my eye I saw this burly black man rushing toward me. He grabbed me and enveloped me in his huge arms.

"This is Rosa's boy," he declared to the throng. "He's our boy. You have to vote for him!"

It was our cook Rosa's husband Arthur coming to my rescue. The place erupted in genuine cheering and applause. Arthur was their "brother" in labor, and his endorsement meant something. If Arthur said it, they would do it.

Of course, in this heavily Asian-influenced city that I grew up in, there were Japanese and Chinese around us. My mother hired Japanese women to do light housekeeping. A Chinese couple that worked for us gave me a little sheepdog named Bushki, who responded only to commands in Chinese, since they had raised him. I didn't just hear the languages; I had to use Chinese to get my dog to sit. So maybe it's not so surprising that I now live in Shanghai, the world's largest city proper. But how different it looks from my original home.

༺ ༺ ༺

I live in a very modern complex of fourteen twenty-four-story towers housing about one thousand residents, mostly Chinese. This residential area is probably greater than all the apartments on San Francisco's Russian Hill put together. At the main entrance gate the ever-present cabs are lined up waiting for customers as people filter out. Each cab company has their own colors (white, pale blue, maroon, gold, dark blue, red), and there are various opinions and stories about which color cab is best. I don't see much difference except in the special cabs that were used at Expo (Shanghai's version of a world's fair, held in 2012), because the drivers who got those cabs were the most experienced and knowledgeable. You can tell by their identity card displayed in the cab which in addition to a photo and number shows stars for duration and quality of service. It is rare to get one with more than one or two stars, but most normal cab drivers have none. The most I've seen is six in an Expo driver's cab, although five is supposed to be the maximum.

I have absorbed my own map of Shanghai in my head and know certain routes for my cab home or walking from place to place. Shanghai is mostly flat so walking is quite enjoyable. There are many nooks and crannies to be explored on almost every block. After my morning coffee, breakfast and run through the stories on the web and overnight emails, I head to the gym. I try to be there at seven, but don't always make it. If I'm not in the gym, at about 8:10 a.m. each weekday morning I hear the loudspeaker from the children's school across the street—the principal starting her morning homily to the students. This is followed by a loud playing of the National Anthem, which can be quite stirring in its march cadence.[4] Sometimes the song isn't sung with the proper gusto so the principal makes the children sing it again.

There is a cultural "jet lag" from the older generation to this one. No easily recalled memories of the hard past to lay out before this young group entering the stream of life. In Shanghai we are all trying to find our path, young and old, newcomer, generational resident. Everything is in flux here but maybe not more so than any of a handful of dynamic cities across the world. Still, old fashioned and contemporary are locked hand in hand. Family, Confucianism, the CCP, social media blocked and unblocked, chic and pitiful, and business always business, money always money, the city revolves around all these things.

Very early each day the blue-clad janitorial crews begin their morning clean up of the front porches and push their large garbage bins to a central garbage collection point. Several tenants walking their dogs pass by. Birds are jumping around the flower beds and the grass and pecking at crumbs and chirping as they go.

As I head out onto my street I get the wonderful experience of observing the ease people seem to have with their surroundings, which almost step-by-step juxtaposes the old and new. Cars stream out of the underground garage and guards open and shut the gates, salute you as you leave, and stop visitors on their way in if they don't know them. Bicycles, motor scooters, grannies pushing baby strollers, and dog walkers are all part of the morning exodus.

Across the street is a very contemporary Thai restaurant; next door to them is an unidentified double-door entrance to somewhere the Thai restaurant's maître d' says is a "place you don't want to go" (which means a massage parlor that isn't). There's a newsstand and the school. Moving down the block are a variety of "hole in the wall" stores that have very helpful and necessary services, including a stationery store/printer, game store, soft goods, cookies and a twenty-four-hour market. I think the last may double as a part-time police station because there always seem to be police motorbikes parked in front and cigarette-smoking policemen in the back room.

At the corner a new residential building called Shanghai One has opened in the past year, and the façade shows that it is mostly a new Kempinski hotel. I am a constant visitor since you can get to my gym through their lobby. There is also a street entrance for the gym down the block where most people go in. I would expect the Kempinski would get a bit irritated if the gym users all used their lobby to enter but I feel pretty comfortable not only because I use the dining room fairly often but also having gotten to know their manager Ms. Karina Ansos, a good German (like the hotel).

It has been interesting watching the hotel struggle in its opening phases through the variations in the dining room staff and management. I got a receptionist from my former gym a job when they opened and the then-manager promised she could learn the system and then move into managing the dining area, which serves breakfast, lunch afternoon tea, and dinner. After about one week her new boss was fired and she was made a waitress. She quit. The next manager lasted about a month and was fired as well. The interesting aspect about him was that he told me the day before he was fired that he had just proposed to his girlfriend in that very restaurant. Poor guy now has no job.

The Shanghai Oriental Notary Public Office is on the opposite corner. Turning from Datian Lu into Fengyang Lu is a natural foods market, two ad hoc hot-food sellers and a few stands for breakfast rolls and patties, dress shops, a "gambling den" open to the street that seems to be mostly Go and card players at very elementary card tables. Next comes the barber, haircuts ¥20 (US $3) pretty good, all scissors. Then come another soft-goods store, a real-estate office, another dress shop, and another office of the Shanghai Oriental Notary Public.

Every weekday a husband and wife team roll out a portable burner and wok with its attached umbrella to cover them and their street visitors. A little dog sleeps at their side, the wife kneading dough and breaking it into palm-sized pieces, pressing it flat; the husband with tongs moves it into the wok conducting with long pincers in baton-like movements, shifting slowly baking thin biscuits, which after a while are moved with precision to a hot plate and stacked up, awaiting the flow of customers. The couple leaves in the early evening.

The spot across the street is filled at night by a noodle and vegetable hot-dinner seller with his portable wok and trickle of late-night clubbers and late-night construction workers. On that side of the street are high-rise buildings including the Kempinski Hotel, a tall office building under construction, and another tall office building with a car dealer, Citibank office, and the ubiquitous Starbucks.

As you stroll along the street you may see a lady pushing a wheelchair with the person in the chair completely covered with a blanket, like a mobile ghost, while the local key maker puts out an advertisement and a chair on the sidewalk to lounge in. Or there might be men pedaling flatbed cycles with three wheels, equipped with bells they ring constantly to let you know they are there and will collect items from you.

In Shanghai, you know you belong when you meet someone on the street whom you know, which for me isn't very often. On the other hand why do I (and others) not make eye contact with other Caucasians when we pass in the street? Is it because we want to be the only outsider here?

There is a new Metro station going up in Jing'an Sculpture Park next to the new Natural History Museum in what the architects call a nautilus shape, and that is close to being finished. The scaffolding is beginning to be removed and the building is emerging in what looks like an innovative design. However I don't know what to make of the façade, with its "squiggly crack lines." The concept was fresh a few years ago but now seems a bit trite. Maybe the time lapse from conception to realization has transformed something unique into something less so but I best wait until the whole presentation is unveiled. China continuously surprises, so I'll give them the benefit of the doubt and see what the final transformation is.

New construction is ever-present in Shanghai and going on in almost every block both here in Puxi and in Pudong. The newly opened Museum of Modern Art in the iconic China Expo Pavilion and the Power Station of Art, a contemporary art museum, are just a few of the civic-related projects just completed.

The little shops along my streets are gradually going "up market" with occasional refurbishing of what are basically concrete box spaces with hanging florescent lights. Not many years ago these same places didn't even have fronts, just open spaces with goods stacked up. You can still see a lot of this down Beijing Xi Lu toward the Bund where various trades dominate each block with plumbing shops all along one side and the next block electrical shops, or siding sellers and so on.

If you step across the street from these shops you can see they are pop-up additions off the fronts of the apartment blocks. This is especially noticeable on Fengxian Lu, where the tree-canopied streets line the blocks outside ornate buildings with exotic statues on the façade. They are now aesthetically ruined by the carbuncles of additions, boxlike stores poking out the front of each building. Along Beijing Xi Lu in my neighborhood, the city has recently removed long blocks of shops and put in small green areas so the buildings behind are now exposed and redone to show their fin de siècle façades.

Of course the neighborhood streets are not empty. There are people of all classes and states of dress mingled together walking down the street to work, coming or going from construction sites, taking the air in ones pajamas, and lining up to buy a breakfast item. Many emerge from the buildings behind the shops that are sort of 1920s buildings with lanes and alleys but not quite the old Shikumen;[5] these are interspersed with taller, old apartment blocks. It is inevitable that these will be knocked down and replaced by gleaming towers like the ones that are already in the neighborhood.

Sweepers are on the job early and seem to be ever-present, keeping things tidy. They are needed and despite refuse boxes, almost every block people still blithely discard wrappers, plastic bottles, and anything else they want to get rid of by throwing it on the sidewalk. However there are many street cleaners who are quite diligent at sweeping up. They are joined from time to time by mini street-cleaning mobile machines that spray water in the cleaned-out trash bins and spots on the curb. These wagons are followed later by those large, water-spraying, spinning-broom machines found in most urban cities. It is a constant effort. This is a big change from years ago when public cleanliness was not a priority. There is often still something to be desired in the public lavatories although they are light-years ahead of what they used to be. And when it comes to graffiti? I think I've seen one rather hasty scrawl, and it was painted over immediately. Taggers couldn't do their damage in the daytime, because there is no such thing as an empty street. If they came in the dead of night, it would be painted over the next morning. The upshot is it's simply not worth doing. Not only risky but futile.

There are several other city workers you encounter walking down the street. The most interesting is the Traffic Assistant as his baseball cap exclaims. He wears his blue official outfit and is found on every block where there are parking meters. He always has a white van with sliding doors parked somewhere in the vicinity; inside the van is a makeshift office with his gathered papers, tea bottle, and an easy chair. When not taking a break he sits curbside in a straight wooden chair and surveys his one-block territory. His target is motorists who want to park. As soon as they begin to park he is on the scene determining how long they will be staying. He then goes to the one parking-meter vending machine found in the middle of the block, pushes a button, and takes the extruded paper to the waiting driver. Now you may ask why the driver can't walk up to the machine himself and tap in his time and get a ticket, but no need. This is a country that has to provide jobs for as many of its citizens as possible.

There are several other useful folks as part of the civic corps of helpers. These people help you cross busy intersections. There are brown-clad, whistle-blowing traffic "policemen" who aren't policemen, hence they are totally ignored by errant, impatient pedestrians. Their only weapon is shame, and they yell or blow a whistle at the person who may or may not then comply. Each corner where these city servants work has a large umbrella he or she can stand under, which also provides a nice shady spot for girls who don't want to get the sun while they wait for the light to change.

At the peak of the rush hour in the morning the street-crossing policemen have an assistant. This person has only a designated jacket with "assistant traffic guide" or something like that. They hold a very small red hand flag and point it in the direction of the green signal to show you are free to cross. Almost all of these assistants appear to be either

Down syndrome-affected or with limited mental skills. It is disturbing and touching to see them diligently pointing their flags as the signals change.

Once you travel the two long blocks down Fengyang you hit the famous Nanjing Xi Lu, one of the most glitzy shopping streets in Shanghai. From then on for about a mile it is almost all tall, modern buildings and international brand stores just as you would see on the world's biggest shopping avenues like Fifth Avenue, Bond Street, or the Ginza, all of whom mimic each other. Fortunately there are a few last-century apartment buildings with their distinct gentle curved façades still on a few corners. Hopefully they will anchor their corners at least for a while.

Close by there is the Line 2 Metro station. There is a constant flow of people in and out of the entrance, which is flanked by the GAP and M&S with large ads as you head for the stairs. Down the stairs you will always find vendors selling jewelry or scarfs and a guy who cleans and puts plastic covers on your mobile phone. Sometimes there is a lone one-string *erhu* player hoping for some coins. If rain threatens, out of nowhere the umbrella salesmen will materialize with a broad display of wares and be quite willing to quote outrageous prices to Westerners until you express a more savvy price, and they will immediately come down. There are always lots of food outlets in the passages to the Metro, often a McDonalds.

Once in the station you may have a few more stands selling magazines or candy and then the entrance itself, which has an airport baggage-scanning device for those with large bundles. This was initiated pre-Expo 2010 and has continued. The buzz is that the company that has the scanning contract here, at all the airports, and with other sites in China was run by Hu Haifeng (胡海峰), the son of former President of China Hu Jintao. When he became the president of Nuctech, a Tsinghua University–owned company, it was granted a near-monopoly by the central authorities and now accounts for about 90 percent of the domestic market. Haifeng has now stepped down probably because the company is under multiple corruption and unfair competition claims from overseas.

My experience on the Metro has been really positive. There are eleven active lines with two more to come shortly and nine more announced. They are clean and efficient, and arrive very regularly; and although they are pretty packed all the time, in my area I usually find a seat within one or two stops. It is quite efficient for getting around especially when heading for Pudong and the symphony during rush hour, when the tunnels can be quite congested. I have two modest caveats. Sometimes the walk between connecting lines is quite long and even in one case you leave the station building and cross the street to an elevated line, and secondly they stop running too early and not universally on all lines or even stations. Usually it is pretty much down by 11 p.m. just when the taxis kick up their meter rates.

Back outside, those who stroll down the streets are of course a mixture of everything and everybody you see in cosmopolitan cities from stunningly attractive Chinese women, Western tourists, and shop girls to the occasional ragged beggar lying on the sidewalk in various grotesque postures.

Panhandling is not practiced by many, but beggars are occasionally found outside a popular tourist destination, restaurant or bar. It appears there is some kind of territorial courtesy because you see the same beggars often at the same place. You also quite often see people scavenging in the trash bins. Not to worry; they apparently make a pretty good living at this.

A man who runs a nonprofit for indigents told me that there is a hierarchy among the street trash-bin scavengers with territory and routes all sorted out. It is apparently quite lucrative for them within this context. To get these people to adopt another lifestyle is a challenge for this nonprofit because they are used to a certain level of income not immediately available for entry-level jobs. They are also reluctant to give up the outdoors.

Another group of people you see on shopping streets are the bicycle vendors. These are the folks who have flatbed carts attached to their bicycles and park them on the widest sidewalks all the while keeping an eye out for the police. The police will ticket them and, I'm told, sometimes actually confiscate their little portable store. Of course the merchants who pay huge rents to have their shops on Nanjing Xi Lu or Huaihai Road hate them.

It is quite humorous to see one as they spot a plainclothes policeman and like a flock of wild geese, flee the scene, furiously pedaling their bikes, only to return minutes later on an adjacent street. Most of them sell cheap purses, scarves, umbrellas, and ripped-off copies of bestsellers.

Always within the group there is one who sells pirated movie DVDs

(¥5/$0.79) or music CDs. To advertise their wares they constantly play the same Mexican love song "¿Quién Será?" It took great effort to find out the name of this song as none of the vendors ever seemed to know, despite playing it day and night. I tried Google, Yahoo, everything I could but never could find what it was. I even got a copy and thought the label would tell me, but the street version has no title. Quite by chance I mentioned it to Vivian Li, who knew of an Apple download called SoundHound that identifies the name of songs by listening as it is played. I downloaded it, moved my iPhone next to the player, and put on my CD. Instantly it identified it. A real marvel of technology. The only exception to everyone playing this song is a vendor outside the magnificent Shanghai Oriental Art Center in Pudong who plays "Starry, Starry Night (Vincent)" over and over, so that you hear it as you enter and leave the hall.

Walking along the streets you pass the motorcycle "taxis," illegal transport found at many central subway exits. They are for very local trips. I've used them once in a while and first you bargain, walk away, bargain, stick to your price (about half the paltry taxi flag-down of ¥14/$2.20 ), and off you go holding on for dear life.

So it is easy to see this part of Shanghai, Jing'An, has a lot of variety, from the Bentley auto-display room to street peddlers and beggars, the high-end restaurants and boutiques, to hole-in-the-wall ladies' fashions. It's all here right before your eyes and ears, and in the distance you hear "¿Quién será? ¿Quién será?" The theme of Expo 2012 was "Better City—Better Life" and signifies Shanghai's new status in the twenty-first century as the "next great world city." What could be better?

**4**. "March of the Volunteers" (Yìyǒngjūn Jìnxíngqǔ 义勇军进行曲) Arise! All those who don't want to be slaves! Let our flesh and blood forge our new Great Wall. As the Chinese people have arrived at their most perilous time. Every person is forced to expel his very last cry. Arise! Arise! Arise! Our million hearts beating as one, Brave the enemy's fire, March on! Brave the enemy's fire, March on! March on! March on! On!

**5**. Shikumen (stone gate) houses are two or three-story townhouses with the front yard protected by a high brick wall. Each residence is connected and arranged in straight alleys, known as a *lòng-tang* (弄堂). The entrance to each alley is usually surmounted by a stylistic stone arch. The whole resembles terrace houses or townhouses commonly seen in Anglo-American countries, but distinguished by the tall, heavy brick wall in front of each house. The literal meaning, "stone gate," refers to the strong gateway to each house.

# Chapter 5

## *City with an Incredible Past*

When I watch the elderly in Shanghai, I find myself imagining all that they have seen. My imagination took off one day and created a character I call Mrs. Yang, a woman born in 1910 in the last breath of the Qing Dynasty. When I first see her, in my mind's eye, I imagine her a young woman in 1937.

Mrs. Yang could hear the turmoil outside her two-story Shikumen. The Japanese soldiers were running in little bunches of three from house to house as the officer in charge looked on from the end of the alley. They had bayonets fixed. They were short, squat, and rumpled; their long rifles jutting out in front of them looked oddly disproportionate.

From her upstairs window spotted with streaks from the cold November rain she could hear Yu Ling, no doubt in her blue and white starched St. Teresa middle-school uniform with pleated shirt and starched blouse with the little crest above her barely discernible breasts, screaming for her mother two homes away. Some soldiers were pulling out furniture and people. Others remained inside, raping.

Mrs. Yang was ready. She had smeared chili sauce over her lower extremities, gotten a dirty dishrag and covered it in hot sauce and stuffed it down her panties. She had changed from her silk cheongsam to mismatched clothing that might be a laborer's outfit. She didn't know if her "bloody" ruse would work and hoped then that the long bayonets would kill her quickly. She wasn't as afraid as much as resigned. She hoped it wouldn't burn like the cut she had gotten just the other day when slicing a mango.

She heard pounding on doors up and down the lane and then suddenly, they reached her door. It wouldn't give. One of the soldiers battered the lock with the butt of his rifle. Nothing. What should she do? Smash, splitting wood, and lots of words scattered with the wood; words that in any language were sure to be curses. They started rummaging in the hall; then they started up the narrow stairs. She was taut, not quivering, but ever so slightly shivering. Up they came, clomping with laced, scuffed brown boots.

Down the alley a shrill whistle blew, then again, again. It reminded her of the sounds when Chiang Kai-shek's thug squads had come in April 1927 looking for Communists to kill. The troops had kept cadence with a constant burst of the whistle. Whenever it stopped, random pillaging would begin again. They paused.

The Manchus had ruled China since 1644, not many years after the Pilgrims first landed on the coast of America. When Mrs. Yang was a little girl, the Qing utterly collapsed, ushering in almost forty years of civic strife. Her parents had lived through invasion as well when Jesus Christ's brother was leading the dreaded Taiping Rebellion. (The Taiping Rebellion was a massive civil war in southern China from 1850 to 1864, against the ruling Manchu Qing Dynasty and led by Hong Xiuquan, who announced that he had received visions in which he learned that he was the younger brother of Jesus.) Hong Xiuquan had attempted to invade the city. Another invasion happened when outsiders had carved Shanghai up with that benign-sounding word "concessions" (a term delivered as casually as if it were a bridge hand). It seems living in Shanghai has always been a tumultuous affair. If it wasn't pirates or local gangsters, it was invaders from all directions. The Taiping army came right outside the city in the 1860s when the colorful American Frederick Townsend Ward and even more colorfully named Ever Victorious Army put a dent in their forces.

She grew up in Shanghai, which itself already had a one-thousand-year history. From the 1840s foreigners lived in appropriated sections of the city. Although she could live there, she was never welcomed. She could not go into many places reserved for Europeans, including some parks and even children's playgrounds.

It is hard for us to fathom today as we enjoy the tranquility of the leaf-canopied former French Concession that this was not an amicable place for Shanghainese. There were separate laws, police, and rules in the three large areas designated foreign concessions. Here the foreign country's rules prevailed. America was a participant. These cutouts of China were leftovers from the two Opium Wars and were codified by what became known as the Unequal Treaties.

When the Qing fell, the Republic of China was formed. But that doesn't mean that there was suddenly a new cohesive government organizing and serving the Chinese people. Power struggles whipped back and forth, and the gangsters, who by the 1920s were a fact of civic life, only encouraged the strife. The Green Gang was a bunch of criminals who ran wild in the International Settlements. The "Paris of the East" as Shanghai was called in the 1920s and for most of the 1930s, was about as tranquil as the real Paris. It was, to put it mildly, a crime-friendly city. If the authorities wanted to really get something done they went to Green Gang boss, Du Yuesheng. "Big-Eared" Du was described by an American observer as "a compound of an Al Capone with social standing, a Lucky Luciano on a Wall Street scale."[6] Shanghai was the leading financial center and largest city in China, if not all of Asia. It was booming and Ms. Yang and her young friends made the most of it.

I thought of her when I visited the Shikumen Open House Museum and picked up a brochure that described how life had been: *a silk cheongsam hangs on the wall; a jade hair clip, red lipstick, rouge, and face powder are neatly laid out on the dressing table. Jazz fills the room as a record is played on the old gramophone, while next door, photographs of old Hollywood movie stars vie for space on walls. You can just imagine the chic lady of the house checking her makeup and hear the rustle of silk as she closes the front door, hails a rickshaw, and heads off to an afternoon tea dance at a city hotel on the Bund.*

Some said, "It was a good time to live in Shanghai ... if you weren't Chinese." That's not entirely true—a certain class of Chinese had a wonderful time in this booming metropolis. As the decade moved into the late 1930s that exuberance fizzled. By the 1940s some parts of China were ruled by warlords, part by Chiang Kai-shek, part by Mao, part by the Western nations and, of course, the Japanese. Their invasion and occupation started in northern China in 1931 and Shanghai in 1937 and didn't end until 1945.

The Japanese justified their invasion of China and the rest of Asia using multiple excuses but primarily they said it was to rid it of foreign devils. Obviously their acts belied their words but looking back from the fifty years after the end of the war they actually may have triggered the vast transformation that took place throughout Asia after World War II. When the Japanese defeated the British in Hong Kong, Malaysia, Singapore, and Burma it shocked the local populace that the white British could be defeated by the yellow local people like themselves. Prior to that, the gospel had been that white armies were superior. The English and French were superior. It turned out they weren't.

This same kind of "blink" may have played a part in the revolution of 1912 in China. The British in 1840 and 1860 with other "white" armies defeated the Qing decisively. This caused the people especially south of the Yangtze to realize that the harsh rule of the Qing was not invincible, and from then on various disruptions took place throughout southern and western China, eventually leading to the fall of the Qing. The Qing were shown not to have heaven's blessing anymore.

I imagine luck on Mrs. Yang's side. The soldiers never made it all the way up her steps. The whistle had blown and immediately the advancing soldiers turned around and left her home. They never came back. The war ended quietly with the surrender of Japan.

But neither Mrs. Yang nor Shanghai were able to settle into a life of harmony and tranquility. When she was just thirty-nine the victorious Red Army marched into Shanghai. Chiang Kai-shek had skedaddled to Taiwan. The civil war ended and New China slowly unfolded its wings from the cocoon of revolution and began to administer itself as a state. Things got worse. When she went out to get staples at the wet market (those are the big open-air markets where everyone shops, for everything from live fish to bok choy) just on the periphery of her Shikumen area, prices had escalated to more than five thousand times what they had been. It was devastating to her little savings. In addition to that, Mao and his new government made some drastic changes to how the country, especially the agricultural sector, was organized.

The Great Leap Forward was in many ways a great leap *backward*, bringing dislocation and starvation. It was an experiment that was supposed to catapult the country forward and instead created a famine that some say caused the death of twenty million people. Mao's policies were beginning to be scrutinized by his fellow leaders, and they didn't like what they saw. By the mid-1960s there was trouble brewing, but Mao as ever outflanked his emerging opponents and unleashed one of the most devastating movements ever to hit a civilized society: the Cultural Revolution.[7]

They arrived at Mrs. Yang's house one afternoon, around 1971, almost as the Japanese had, an unruly, frantic, shouting mob of teenagers and a handful of recent university students. They yelled slogans, carried signs denouncing "Capitalist Roaders" (meaning those who would lead the Chinese down a capitalist road) and other fabricated enemies of Mao's vision for a utopian China, cleared of all the remnants of the civilization that had preceded it. All objects of historical memory were smashed. Churches turned into warehouses. Homes like Mrs. Yang's were appropriated. The "masses" were now ruling, although in truth it was out of control schoolboys, sycophants, and the ever-present opportunists who knew to jump onto a good thing when they saw it.

They pounded on her door and demanded she open it. When she did they yanked her by the hair into a little semicircle that was formed to denounce her corrupt ways of having a home that could serve at least four families and yet was only housing her. They pushed her aside and took what they wanted. They smashed ceramic figurines given to her by her late uncle, who had been recently beaten to death by roaming bands of "patriots." She tried to protest and this just got her punched. She couldn't defend herself; she was in her sixties and already somewhat frail, thanks to a bad diet and lack of adequate medical care.

That week three families moved into her house. She was allocated a top-floor room, but the rest of the house was out of her control. A neighborhood committee kept an eye on things and pulled her out weekly for indoctrination and self-criticism gatherings. Society as it had been known even under the dreaded occupation was not as harsh as this. She barely survived. A distant cousin would come about once a month and try to help out and always brought a few fresh clandestinely procured vegetables. They kept her going.

This chaos lasted from 1966 to 1976 and only ended with Mao's death and the arrest of his wife and the rest of the Gang of Four.

A new president was appointed but soon elbowed aside. How many more changes could Mrs. Yang, now in her seventies, take? She still faced one more jolt. The "Little Bottle" Deng Xiaoping—his nickname stemmed from the literal meaning of his last name—one of Mao's early successors now famously proclaimed, "I don't care if it's a white cat or a black cat. It's a good cat as long as it catches mice."

The world swung topsy-turvy. What had been bad was now good. The message was clear. "Get going, make your own life. Live your dreams." Deng Xiaoping's cat quote, although uttered in a speech in the 1960s, was used now in the 1970s with "to get rich is glorious" (致富光荣), unleashing an almost total reversal of the previous years. By the time Deng stepped aside in 1980 the ratchet of change transformed, once again, the society and Shanghai with it.

The squatter families who had moved in her home moved out. She was once again alone in her home. Prices stabilized; Shanghai roused itself to yet another new life.

With my mind's eye I last saw Mrs. Yang, standing on the promenade at the Bund watching fireworks with some of her cousin's children. Her eyes sparkled even without the bursts from the exploding fireworks.

6. *Old Shanghai: Gangsters in Paradise* by Lynn Pan
7. The Great Proletarian Cultural Revolution took place from 1966 to 1976. Mao alleged that bourgeois elements were infiltrating the government and society at large, aiming to restore capitalism. He insisted that these revisionists be removed through violent class struggle. China's youth responded to Mao's appeal by forming Red Guard groups around the country. Millions of people were persecuted in the violent factional struggles that ensued across the country, and suffered a wide range of abuses including public humiliation, arbitrary imprisonment, torture, sustained harassment, and seizure of property. After Mao's death in 1976, reformers led by Deng Xiaoping gained prominence. Most of the Maoist reforms associated with the Cultural Revolution were abandoned by 1978. The Cultural Revolution has been treated officially as a negative phenomenon ever since.

# Chapter 6

## *The Great Leap Backward*

In Xi'an, my guide at the Museum of Qin Terra-Cotta Warriors and Horses told an incredible story about her childhood during the Great Famine of 1958 to 1961. Her grandfather with whom she lived "because my parents didn't like me" used to get her up at three in the morning to go fishing. It was pitch dark and cold, but this was the only way to provide food. Grandfather had a big fishing rod, which she helped him carry, and they would trudge off toward a local muddy river. Her job was to dig a hole and fill it with water so they could throw in the fish and keep them alive. This was hard work for a little girl. Her hands were almost numb with the watery cold.

One time her grandfather snagged a fish that was so big he had to jump into the water to try and capture it. He couldn't hold on. It was very discouraging. Usually after about an hour they caught enough for the one meal for the day and walked back home where she snuggled back into bed and slept until morning. Her other chore was to collect edible bugs using a long blade of grass. Confident today, sixty-plus years later she could still identify a "good bug" from a bad one. "Good" meant edible and used as cooking oil since they couldn't afford to buy oil or, for that matter, even much salt.

Her grandfather had been one of Mao's guards, but ended up in poverty and later during the Cultural Revolution was ostracized, all his mementos destroyed. His infraction was that his father and grandfather had been landowners and hence he was a "Capitalist Roader" and to be despised. She didn't say if he was actually beaten, but he became a recluse for the rest of his life.

She was a cheerful woman, and her son was embarking that very week on the vast national test to try to gain admission to Xi'an University. Her sisters were doctors, and she had become a nurse but loved history so much she took up guiding at the terra-cotta warriors museum. This is only one family's story but gives us just a glimpse of what happened to families high and low. Some of the big cities like Shanghai were not in such dire circumstances as the countryside but none were unscathed.

One of the causes of the famine was that local officials who were given a quota for food production wouldn't dare report they did not meet their quota. The central government, then believing that the local authority had met the target, would require a percentage of the quota to be sent to the central authorities. Because of the false reporting they took out a huge percentage of the actual production, leaving little for the local population. People starved by the millions.

The early days of New China were built on false ideology and science. Mao thought collective farms were the socialist answer to produce and distribute food to the vast population so that everyone got their fair share. Of course this was forced on those who tended small plots, and production plummeted. At the same time the Great Leap Forward was having others build backyard "steel mills" and melting their pots and pans to meet other quotas. In many cases you ended up not only lacking food but a wok to cook any food you had. This was all part and parcel of Mao's idea that China could leapfrog out of an agrarian society to an industrial one if only they just harnessed the capacity of the common people. Nobody really knows how many people died.

Recently I was told something quite riveting. Despite this history, some older people wish they could go back to the Mao days. Huh? This can't be true! Their explanation is that during the days from the founding of the New China in 1949 to the death of Mao in 1976 every one was considered equal or at least that was the intention. Factory workers and modest laborers felt they were the same social level as someone who worked in an office or was an official. Some had advantages others didn't, but in general it was as leveled a society as can be reasonably attained. However that all changed when Deng Xiaoping initiated economic reforms.

Factories were closed because they weren't making a profit and people found themselves out of a job for the first time in their lives. Some began to prosper in the new environment, while others felt they were diminished and not on the same plane as those who had better jobs. As society realigned itself there were those who longed to be respected again. Longed to be equal. Such a natural impulse. Maybe this is a tiny ember that jolted the leadership when Bo Xilai—the now discredited party chief in Chongqing—was having old Mao songs sung and plays revived. No doubt many in the leadership in Beijing were apoplectic. The day after they arrested Bo, Wen Jiabao, premier of the state council, said that China was on a very thin edge between advancing and falling back into the cataclysm of the Cultural Revolution days. Yet today there are still some older people that think of Mao's regime as "the good old days." Clearly most people I talk to don't think this way, but the power of those utopian ideas still resonates.

# Chapter 7

## *Like Finding Your Way in a Thick Fog*

There can be many frustrations involved with living in a foreign city. Here are a few examples of the strange complications of Shanghai, starting with the most basic: taking a trip to the bank.

There are ATMs almost everywhere in and outside banks, for the most part telephone-booth style—where you can slide a lock to enter. Most of the ATMs seem to limit you to withdrawing a certain amount of RMB each event, but will allow you to take your card out and do it again several more times. For example you may type in you want to withdraw ¥5000; so you click it but it says No, you can't. Okay, how about ¥2,500 twice? No, you can't do that either. How about ¥2,500 and then ¥2,000, and then again ¥500—whirr and out it comes. I'm not sure of the logic, but it works. This is only a precursor to the turmoil that awaits you to do banking face to face.

In many countries banking is done over the Internet or even on your cell phone. I couldn't get along living outside the United States without my online bill-pay account. Not only can I pay my bills; they can be automatically scheduled and all other banking needs taken care of. From time to time I transfer funds to China so I can pay my local bills using my bank, China Merchants.

Indicative of how things work, their website has an English version for everything, except what you need it for, i.e., to pay bills. That part is only in Chinese. What's the solution? Vivian Li helped me to screen-save the page, which we then printed and she wrote English next to the Chinese instructions. She then entered the banking site and typed out in Chinese characters my usual bills and all the information that goes with them. Screen-save, print, translate. So now all I have to do to pay my rent or Ayi, my housekeeper, or anyone else is put in the amount after clicking several empty spaces, which pop up the Chinese characters, and when I'm all done, click 出口.

One additional complication is that I use an Apple MacBook, and the bank website will only recognize Windows. The solution is that I have an old Dell with Windows and use that exclusively for online banking.

What if you have to go to the actual bank to take care of a transaction? Woe to he who enters wanting to get something done. Ever been in a "take a number" government office? You got it. Rows of "airport" benches facing a glassed-in area where six or so clerks can handle your affairs as you try to communicate through the opening in the glass partition. You shove your passport (needed for almost anything), your bank card, your other ID, and the reason for the visit. Of course this is all theoretical, as the six tellers are never there. Maybe there are two, and you can exasperatingly see the others chatting, eating, talking on the phone, but above all, not helping you.

Early on I got a bank debit card and was using it after I had sent about US $25,000 for deposit in my local account. The clerk swiped my card and it was rejected. "Insufficient funds." What? I didn't have sufficient funds in my RMB account for a small purchase. How was this possible after I just made a large deposit? Easy: Chinese banks don't automatically take wired funds into your RMB account without you coming in, taking a number, giving your passport, explaining in only partially understood English what you want, and on and on.

Once they have established the wait has been long enough and the girl at the teller's window has ruffled through your information, she informs you she can't do it. You have no funds.

"No, miss, I do have the money in the account.... *Your bank* sent me a notice on my mobile phone. Look!"

Oh! she says. Click, click, click.

"You can't do it."

This time she informs me that under Chinese law I can only transfer US $50,000 in any one year without multiple forms and testimonials. *"But I have only transferred US $40,000 this year."*

Click, click, click, she leaves her chair, gets someone else to help her, click, click, click. She goes away again. Comes back. Sign here.

It's like a stage show filled with multiple actors, pantomime, indolence, gesticulation, exasperation, the depression of failure, the thrill of success, all in little more than an hour. They ought to sell tickets for each performance.

Months later I return, having transferred another slug of money. I take a number and look at rows of people waiting, tellers not telling, hours ahead. Revolt! I can't stand it. I walk over to a part of the bank that has three very prim, identically dressed, perfectly coifed MBA-looking young ladies shuffling papers. I go to the first assuming she must be some sort of supervisor and ask why she doesn't get some more tellers working? With a bright smile and in perfect English she says something like "I have no jurisdiction over the (lazy incompetent) tellers."

"Okay," I say, "You do it for me." There's a slight hedge; she looks down, pauses, and gives a bright smile. "Hmmm," she says. "I think we have a new machine that can do it for you."

Over we go to a machine standing all alone in the lobby. "Let's see your bank card." Tap, tap, done! Money transferred. Printed receipt. I asked her to marry me to insure that she will be here next time. She wasn't.

China respects age. Even coming into immigration at the airport there is a special line I can go through without waiting. When Expo 2010 was on and seventy-four million visitors came, huge lines ensued. Not for me. Anyone over seventy or in a wheelchair could go in a VIP side-door. There was no waiting. You could even bring a companion with you, ostensibly your "nurse" or helper. Shanghai has its rascals and some people admitted to the VIP gates in wheelchairs were cured the instant they passed through them, rising from the chairs and walking about; it was better than Lourdes. This caused some public outcries, especially from those who had waited in line for hours. Fixes were instigated, organizers huffed and puffed, and new rascals found ways in.

Proving my age involves some explaining. The Chinese would show their Identity Card.[8] Whenever I offer up my California driver's license it causes confusion until I point out where my date of birth is printed. By regulation foreigners are supposed to carry their passports at all times, but no one I know does so. For a while I carried a photocopy in case I was stopped.

Once in Singapore I was asked to show my ID at a movie theater when I was buying a ticket. I told the sales clerk I wouldn't unless he explained what he'd be using it for. He gave in and sold me a ticket.

I've stopped bothering with the photocopy of the passport. Apparently if you are stopped you suffer only the consequence of a little lecture. From time to time the government makes big announcements that they going to crack down but this is aimed at those who overstay their visas. The "cracking down" lasts about a week or two and they seem to know beforehand where these overstayers congregate.

But if I wanted anonymity and personal space, I certainly came to the wrong place. How does 3,500 years of civilization, a modern, state-dominated economy, and 1.3 billion people affect your day-to-day life in China? Some of the 1.3 billion people are always bumping into you, jostling you, blocking the Metro doors or elevator, trying to come in while you are trying to get out. There is little sense of "giving way" when getting into a restaurant, movie, food stall.

There is no guile in shoving the person making a request in front of you while you are transacting already, say at the train ticket window. Queuing has not been perfected by the average older Chinese. They blithely force their way into the line and start talking to the ticket agent you are already doing business with. It doesn't matter that you are already there carrying on a transaction; you don't exist. You soon learn a little elbow or blocking motion temporarily keeps them at bay. "No offense, lady, but I will knock you down if you don't back off," you think. You do your best to block her on the way from the counter so the next person moves up as they should.

Yet at some places lines seem to form and be quite orderly, at, say, Starbucks, or if ropes have been set up. You may not have to scrum at every ticket counter or dumpling outlet. You also learn to wait in a loose queue. That is a line that isn't a line, but sort of is, like the lines to show your boarding pass when getting on a plane.

Privacy at public places, even in the midst of a transaction, is an unknown state of affairs. Thank goodness ATMs have doors that lock. Can you imagine if they didn't?

People don't expect privacy as we Westerners know it. Standing in a Metro subway train there are multiple conversations almost always going on at various decibels. Passengers shouting over the phone (no doubt the logic of this being that the other person is far away) is just everyday stuff. No one seems to mind and no one reacts. Maybe the conversations are just boring or they are soap operas in progress. Hey, don't get off! I want to hear what's next.

What does happen on the Metro quite often is that I'm offered a seat by young and old. It is really quite common, and although I think I don't look old to others maybe I look like a guy who could use a seat. I am always very touched that so many, in quite crowded trains, spontaneously get up and offer me their seat.

Another "get used to it" aspect of Shanghai? Crowds. Every street, avenue, and boulevard has people walking, jostling you, pushing by, bumping into your arm. At first you want to say, "excuse me" if you inadvertently touch someone but very soon realize this is just normal. Everyone bumps everyone without a pause. That's just the way it is with so many people.

This flow of people is especially evident in train stations—not only in the waiting areas where people are seated as far as you can see but when you head for a train. People flow like salmon heading upriver to spawn; only they are going down corridors and stairways until they reach their destination. Great flows of humanity are evident in the city, especially on holidays in certain "magnet" areas, such as Nanjing Dong Lu, a walking street with shops on every side. It is a sea of black hair.

During these holidays it is actually much easier to cross town in a cab, because lots of the temporary residents have gone elsewhere, maybe back to their home villages. The tourists tend not to go to the residential areas where my friends and I live, so it is amazingly uncrowded during festivals and holidays. Remove about six million from the equation by sending them out of town, and it makes a difference.

With so many people everywhere how does this affect crossing the street? How do you cross the street? Very carefully! When the light changes to "walk," you don't. You wait, pause, look both directions, and then join the crowd for protection.

Here a "zebra" crossing is no doubt a sighting mechanism helpful to cars running you down. Green means you might be able to get across if traffic on the left stops. The inner lane can make a right turn without even pausing even though they are staring at a red light. Cars that are turning left on the green can zoom through the crosswalk as can the cars in the same direction turning left. Are you confused?

There are at least three streams of traffic to watch for and, oh yes, the motor bikes and bicycles may or may not pay attention to the green and slip through in any direction without a pause, whether on the street or on the curb. Traffic lights go green, yellow, red, and red, yellow, green. Yellow means to cars "get going." Red means motorbikes keep going and dodge and weave through the rest of traffic, which also ignores the change of lights for the first few seconds if they see no obstacle. Pedestrians don't count to drivers. In all cases: pedestrian beware.

Buses will roar through and threatening to run you down when the light is green for you. And yes, in all of this horns are honking, motorbikes chugging, and bicycles ringing bells or not. Those on bicycles may be totally oblivious to everyone else and just pedal between you and the curb. No one ever seems to give a thought to going around you.

Who has the legal right of way? Come on, that is a little like saying I'll take you to a Chinese court, just before the other party guffaws in hysterical laughter.

It takes the "convoy" system to cross a street that has no traffic light. You wait until a crowd gathers, then all cross at once, defying the traffic to kill you all. The newspapers reported that even with signals people are unwilling to wait more than about a minute and a half before trying to cross. Some signals are as long as two minutes. Most have numbers showing when there is twenty seconds to go and a countdown ensues.

An interesting aspect of crossing the street was a system devised to show pedestrians that they should obey the signal instructions. Apparently this was initiated when "walk" signs were first installed. The corner traffic attendant held a small red flag in his hand, and when he saw someone not observing the crossing lights he handed them the flag. They in turn could only get rid of it by giving it to someone else who was ignoring the rules. Sort of capture-the-flag and tag rolled into one. I wish I had been around to see it. Can you imagine the confusion, humiliation, rejection, and confrontations it caused? I was told it worked for the short time they tried it and got people to follow the street crossing lights. Sometimes.

꿈 꿈 꿈

At the Kempinski Hotel I've mentioned, there have been several complete staff turnovers and even the restaurant-management company, a local, well-known group, was kicked out or left. The hotel then took over. They seem now to have it in hand, although the waitstaff still changes regularly. I have managed to befriend the chef, Matthias, so he no longer sears my eggs or unduly uses oil. I have been unsuccessful in getting them to turn off the awful music in the morning, and I have made no headway in getting the ever-changing staff to give me the correct method to connect to the wifi.

"How do I connect to your wifi?" I ask.

They give me a code for guests in the hotel. I tell them that I am not a guest in the hotel.

The next response is "Oh, then I don't know how to do it" instead of "Let me find out how."

This is very illustrative of many people when asked to solve a query.

When I was running my company this was a lesson that needed to be taught over and over, and really, unless the person is so inclined, it is a futile effort. They try to answer the immediate inquiry.

"Go check this with Mr. So and So."

Later they report back that he is not around. Instead of solving the problem of getting the inquiry answered. I think of it as just jumping over the first hurdle and moving on until you cross the finish line. Most people see the hurdle and turn around.

Much of the day-to-day staff you run into is not from Shanghai. As I have mentioned, there are an amazing six million "immigrants" (as they are called here) doing everything from construction to waiting on tables. There is a sort of oblivion to proper behavior. The other day I was showering after working out at my gym. There I was soaping and washing when my shower curtain was yanked aside and the guy responsible for cleaning the shower area shot his cold water hose at the floor drain. Now what the hell was he thinking? I'll guess. He had a job. It was to clean the showers. If people were using a particular shower stall it didn't occur to him to clean the many empty ones first. You might think he was a complete blockhead, but no doubt in his mind he was just doing what he was told. Clean the showers. No one had explicitly told him not to bother the people in the showers or do it at a time no one is showering. With most of us that would go without saying. Well, I guess if you don't say it, people just don't get it.

The men's locker room is inevitably in disarray and not cleaned from the day before. Overflowing trash bins, old wet rags on the sink, dirty bathroom, even a hose stretched into the shower area. I've complained, like the foreign devil I am, and the manager's assistant, who is the only English speaker, said they would get the janitor to come in before seven. And indeed in subsequent days he did. Did he clean the locker room? No. He mopped the floor by the boxing ring and areas unused by anyone.

Again this was pointed out to the manager's assistant, and she said she would get him to attend to the locker rooms first. Days pass and no change. Janitor again reminded. No change. By chance I was changing when he came in a few days later. He was eating an apple and put his hand in the trash bin and moved the stuff around, all the while holding a new plastic bag which normally would be used to change the wastebasket. Nothing done. Then he proceeded to wipe the sink area with an ugly rag and leave it on the counter. He proceeded into the shower area and sat down while his bucket sat in a shower and a hose coiled on the floor. He then left. At least he didn't turn the hose on me again.

Back to the assistant manager. "He thinks it is like his own home and that's what he does at home," she concludes. He is just doing what he knows how to do. Orderliness and cleanliness aren't high on the priority list. I spoke to the manager of the Kempinski, which uses the same gym as their "in-house" facility, and it is driving her crazy; German precision meets China's far more casual policy of "it looks OK to me."

A fellow I know runs a very busy chocolate-cake shop, and he says his greatest challenge is personnel. Not only is there high turnover but you can train them carefully on what to do but may not be aware of what they don't know to do. What normal things you may expect anyone to know they may not know and you don't find out until a customer complains. Even if they complain directly to the staff, the staff doesn't understand what is bothering them. I saw this in a sandwich shop where I know the sandwich makers are supposed to wear plastic gloves when they prepare food. I watched as a food preparer made this guy's sandwich and when he finished took off the gloves and picked up the sandwich and struggled putting it in its paper wrapping, of course defeating the whole purpose of wearing the gloves in the first place. The customer complained and refused the sandwich, and honestly the sandwich maker didn't have any understanding of the complaint. He had done what he was instructed and that was to wear gloves when making a sandwich. No one had explicitly said not to take them off when you are placing it in its wrapping.

My own annoyance is when clerks give you your change or an item you have purchased, they most often don't look at you and either offer it to you as they gaze elsewhere or literally toss it on the counter as if you aren't there. By experience I have become a bit used to it and am told that it is just usual. No offense. We're done, so "next." Why waste time making eye contact or smiling? Is this indifference or "you're not my family, so why should I care about you" or nothing more than just the way things are done?

Sometimes while walking you will see someone throw a wrapper on the pavement and just walk on, even if there are rubbish bins at the street corner. Is it the concept of "not my job" since there are constant waves of blue-clad sweepers coming down the street each day with their spindly straw branch brooms (no doubt left over from a witch's flight)? Is the logic "It's not my house, so who cares?"

Others have pointed out that there is a very close mental construct that separates *my* family from the rest of humanity. What do I care if you are in front of me in line or getting out of the Metro or trying to catch an elevator as the "close door" button is feverishly pushed? To an outsider this seems like multiple manifestations of pure selfishness or at least just bad manners. To an insider maybe it just makes sense. I can't be responsible for the other 1.3 billion people. I have to take care of my family and myself. No one else is of interest to me. I don't need to acknowledge that others may be inconvenienced by my actions. What matters are my family and me.

Now clearly this observation is not entirely true for all, and there are a great number of folks who show generosity of spirit in acts of civic virtue all the time, but I must say there is something overall that seems to be missing or maybe more precisely there is a different mental construct.

But not all that is lost in translation is negative: it seems odd to us that a waiter will stay by your table while a decision is made about what to eat. But they are there to give advice and answer questions about dishes no matter how long it may take you to make up your mind.

Another area of frequent "overservice" in a service economy involves real-estate agents. While agents may be despised the world over, the ones I've encountered here have been quite positive and helpful. Unlike the way it works in America, the Chinese real-estate agents are nonexclusive; they expect you to have two or three working on the same project at the same time. I've noticed a similar thing in art galleries. You can visit multiple galleries and they will have many of the same artists. In the West the galleries I've known have exclusive distribution of an artist's work and in turn help promote the artist. Here that is not the norm and the client gets not only a variety of work but prices as well.

In terms of public behavior there seems to be recognition that there is room for improvement. Signs have gone up in bus stations that say "voluntarily queue up." And one of my favorites: "Be civilized." This is part of something called Queue Day, which falls on the eleventh of each month.

There also seems to be a little "toilet training" going on. As the *Global Times* put it in a recent article: "Residents who forget to flush will now be reminded to be kind to fellow public toilet users by quotes from pop-song lyrics." I don't know if this means they will install music in the public toilets, but it might be an improvement.

There is also a campaign to get people to stop shouting into their cell phones in public places. In keeping with this, the same article that mentions the toilets states: "It is the latest attempt by municipal authorities to improve the behavior of the capital's citizens by thinking up new slogans that are more appealing to a modern age. Tang Zhihua, from the Beijing Municipal Party Committee, told the *Global Times* Thursday that by March next year, there will be one hundred thousand of the new signs on display in public places, including shops, airports, hotels, and residential communities. Tang, who is the director of the publicity department of the society construction work-office under the committee, said that Beijing is still not as civilized as is desired. The move to introduce the new mottos in more public places will make it easier for the public to receive guidance about any potential bad behavior, he said. They are less preachy in tone, which is why trendy words and song lyrics have been used. 'I don't think bad behavior will disappear if the slogans have bossy wordings,' said Tang." You got that right, Mr. Tang.

My conclusion is that China has some harsh characteristics and some gentle ones. The government seems to be aware of some of the behavior that needs attention. In the meantime, it's up to me to adapt and be aware and flexible.

---

**8**. The Resident Identity Card (居民身份证) is the official form of personal identification carried by all Chinese.

# Chapter 8

## *My Special Places*

After some time in Shanghai I began to establish a few places in the city I like to return to when the mood and weather cooperate.

At People's Square there is an English-speaking corner, which is a gathering spot each Sunday. Young and old together bushwhack Westerners who are strolling by, so they can try out their English. It is quite a swirl of people and one day I encountered a group that included at least three children about seven, one of whom was amazingly fluent. Their teacher was with them and justifiably very proud.

The English speakers are always a mix of kids, students in high school and university, plus one or two businessmen. The older businessmen often try to take over the conversation to show how good they are, and it takes some tact to try and get them to let others speak. One Sunday there was a lady from the Bank of China that asked for a complete explanation of how the Federal Reserve Bank works and a young man who had just been admitted to Stanford Business School. The group totally encircles you; I have to constantly turn in small half circles to try to include everyone.

Once, while we were talking, a storm broke and we adjourned under a tented area that apparently was prepared for just such a thing. We carried on with thunder, lightning, and a torrential downpour. About one hour I was exhausted from answering questions. They all knew and liked Obama and even without prompting quoted his favorite saying. "Yes, we can" and "Turn the page." Quirkily enough, not far from the park is a market named the Obama Market.

Near to the English-speakers corner is a very unique gathering—parents who are advertising their son or daughter as an eligible marriage partner. Every weekend there are close to fifty or more people sitting along a long wall, which is completely plastered with "résumés" of the eligible candidates. There seems to be some order to it; all the signs are about the same size and format and almost always include a photograph. Lurking close by the paper presentation is someone to inform you of the finer points of a person you might be inquiring about. Phone numbers and emails are freely posted. Onlookers slowly scan the offers, browse, and chat. The strange system must work; otherwise everyone wouldn't show up every weekend.

The park is quite extensive, including four museums, lots of cultivated flowers, trees, and a large pond populated by beautiful floating lotus. One of the main Metro hubs is directly under your feet and thousands of people will be passing through any time you are there. On various sides of the park are some of the oldest and newest buildings in Shanghai. It is really the one of the centers for leisure. There is a tall clock tower, the last remaining structure from another era when the whole area was a racetrack.

The museums in People's Park have a very specific charm. The Shanghai Museum of Art is a classic building with lots of marble interior and sweeping staircases. Today it is used mainly for special exhibitions. The building has a good feeling to it and in a way is how you imagine a museum ought to look. Very close by is a small modern art museum with lots of glass walls, incorporating the woodland aspect of the park into the museum experience. It hosts many special exhibits as well. Both museums have been somewhat preempted by the newly opened modern art museum in the iconic China Pavilion building in Pudong and a contemporary museum called the Power Station, which is—like the Tate Modern—in an old power station. When I'm in the mood for ancient Chinese art I can visit yet another museum in the park, the Shanghai Museum, which is built in the shape of an ancient bronze cooking pot.

During "good weather," which means in spring and autumn, I take at least one day a week and explore by walking around near or far. It is very informative to just take a walk without a predetermined agenda and see what appears. Sometimes I pick a part of the city or a special park and take the Metro and then walk the area.

Good weather also means that the pollution level isn't too overpowering. Pollution in Shanghai is not the stifling problem it is in Beijing but indeed there are very few immaculately clear, blue-sky days. Often it is just a vague haziness that fortunately doesn't seem to descend to building level. Not far outside the city you sometimes run into the dreaded pollution clearly visible at street level. It is almost a fog.

Shanghai is extremely varied and the most interesting sites aren't necessarily right along the main thoroughfares. Many alleys, called *lòng-tang* (弄堂), provide exciting excursions. One such excursion led me to an old Catholic church right in the middle of an old complex. I gingerly pushed open the front door and climbed the stairs to find a labyrinth of offices and corridors, finally leading to a bright open room that turned out to be the main church altar and assembly room.

While I was trying to find my way back I kept being thwarted by doors nailed shut and blocked passageways. I couldn't find my way out. I did see some dimly lit offices and there seemed to be people around, but I wasn't confident of sign-language "Chinese" so didn't know how to ask the route out. Just then a Chinese friend from the United States called and I told her my predicament. This engendered great amusement on her end. Nevertheless she agreed to help me find my way. I did so by disturbing one of the occupants of a dimly lit room. He was startled to see me and even more startled when I handed him my phone. Shortly my friend's voice did its magic and he took on the role of solicitous companion, leading me down a stairway to the sunshine.

Initially I lived on Hengshan Lu in one of the concession areas, Xuhui, still today familiarly called the French Concession, which it used to be. This area turned out to be most charming and especially interesting since it contains many of the last remaining free-standing homes from the turn of the century, plus historical homes of Sun Yat Sin (in China called Sun Zhongshan (孫中山));[9] his wife Soong Ching Ling, one of the famous Soong sisters and honorary president of China; former Premier and Foreign Minister Zhou Enlai (周恩来); Chiang Kai-shek, called Jiǎng Zhōngzhèng (蔣中正), whose wife was also a Soong sister, Soong May-ling, and others. These are interlaced with old and new buildings and Shikumen. To show you how times change, the wedding and first home of Chiang Kai-shek and Soong Mei-ling (宋美齡), known the world over as Generalissimo and Madame Chiang Kai-shek, is now a restaurant and bar. Up one of the stairways the lone reminder is the copy of their wedding photo. *Sic transit gloria mundi.*

Not far from my former apartment there is a cluster of homes set in the middle of the square block with limited access from the street. The houses face perpendicular to the only two lanes where cars can fit, so they become walking streets with a wonderful quiet tranquility in the middle of this busy city. The homes are two- and three-story duplexes, surrounded by lots of foliage and all with front yards with little fences. I wonder if it is public or private housing but know it would be a delight to live in such an area. These homes appear as if they were built over the last five or ten years, not like the congested blocks of Shikumen areas—very, very weathered old two- and three-story brick housing found intermittently throughout the city but which are gradually being cleared away for large apartment complexes.

There is another small street south of the same area that has a wonderful sprinkling of small restaurants and shops. This leads to a much more active road that brings you to the Shanghai Museum of Arts and Crafts. This museum is a combination craft exhibits with the craftspeople actually there doing their painting, weaving, pottery, etc., and a store where much of the exhibit material is for sale, not copies but originals. That makes "museum" a bit of a stretch, but there are some exhibit materials that aren't for sale. One of the best parts of the whole thing is the house itself, which initially looked to me as a small version of the White House. It has been through various lives including a legation. Today's use seems perfect, especially with the added attractions of a few wandering cats and a very lovely garden.

It is really fun to come upon interesting streets and venues. I also walked right by a restaurant that I'd been trying to find for months but that had proved impossible to find by cab, even though it turned out to only be a few blocks from me. It is called the Peace Mansion and used to be a former general's home. Diagonally across the street is a popular restaurant run by a fellow San Franciscan, called GoGa, short for Golden Gate.

When you walk down Wulumuqi Lu toward Huaihai Lu you pass very young Red Army guards, at attention outside the American Consulate complex and its next-door neighbor, the Iranian Consulate, which is across from the French. The neighborhood geography seems to suggest "let's be friends." The Chinese guards are very polished and at strict attention with their heads smoothly turning left and right to scan the block, however I noticed that from time to time there is a slight variation as an especially attractive girl walks past. They become completely flummoxed when a passing visitor stops and asks them directions. They are guards, can't talk, can't engage in eye-to-eye contact—"Go away" their body language says—but indeed they will very stiffly say something, which I interpret, quite possibly incorrectly, to be "get lost, I'm on duty." That's certainly what it looks like.

Sometimes after working out at a gym on Huaihai I'd walk a few blocks to a street-seller area with outdoor and semi-indoor shops, all filled with fruits and vegetables, fish swimming in buckets, and many hot items just off the griddle. A few steps away is a vendor selling steaming hot dumplings.

The sidewalks in this area have been pulled up and replaced with brick, which seems to sit on sand without any sealant. When the workmen pound the bricks they settle into place without any unevenness; somehow this system works. Several spots along a long street will be left undone as the bricks have to be cut to size later to fit exactly. They put a slightly different color here and there, and it adds to the finished look of the sidewalk.

Down the block I once saw a gathering of the ever-present street-sweeper brigade all lined up emptying the contents of their carts to a central garbage truck. It was quite nice to see, all of them wearing powder-blue outfits and using brooms made from tree branches, looking for all the world like witches' broomsticks.

࿊ ࿊ ࿊

Living in Shanghai it is not unusual to see construction: low-rises going down, high-rises going up, empty space filled up with new buildings or small parks, just the way of a growing modern city reconstituting itself. The only breather for all this constant activity was in 2010 during Expo, when all was suspended.

I live in a relatively quiet area in Jing'An across from the lovely Jing'An Sculpture Garden where the new anthropology museum is being constructed among the wonderful blooming trees, rows of flowers, and interactive sculpture. Lots of grannies and their little toddlers come every day after the early morning exercisers and joggers are gone.

A small, lovely old street called Fengxian begins near here, sprouting off Fengyang Lu, and curves to parallel Nanjing Xi Lu.

In my years of living in this neighborhood I've made a point to walk by Fengxian at least once a day. I have become so entranced that I've photographed it in every season, and even at night. Very few cars ever came down the street, just bicycles and motorbikes moving to the rhythm of a far-off signal. The street has a very gentle curve.

On one side of the street there are robust bushes hemmed by a tapering grass that hugs the side, and everything is guarded by very ancient trees. The highest branches interlace the neighboring trees in a broken canopy of greenery and sunshine, just the kind you see reflected in so many artist's canvases of sun-dappled pathways. It has a special harmony in both setting and presence. Or it had. Because it simply doesn't exist anymore.

A brand-new version has appeared one hundred meters east of the old street. New pavement, curbs, curves, trees, signs, and a four-way stop signal, which anticipates a constant flow of autos. The old charm is gone, for now. After one last glimpse, the road and trees gone. A gate now blocks the past.

Why was it moved? The only explanation that is credible is that by moving the street there is now a large parcel of land without the street intersecting it. I can't imagine this being done anywhere else, where people decide to just move the street because they need, or want, some more land. I'm sure something of civic value has been achieved and a new glimmering building will soon arise on the now-cleared dirt where the old road was, but the harmony and quiet, canopied dignity now lives only in the memory of those who used to pass through it each day.

At least Jing'An Sculpture Park remains intact. I live just across the street from this welcoming little oasis, which opens at 5 a.m. Even then people begin to seep into it. Many head for the part of the park that has a cork-like surface, inviting because it is easy on the feet. They walk, run, and guide people in wheelchairs. I often watch the early morning flow as it continues to build. By 6 a.m. people gather, ready to be led in morning exercises set to music, with the freelance instructors using microphones to beef up their instructions. There are multiple sessions, one after another, and sometimes even simultaneously with competing instructors.

By about 8 a.m. everyone is gone except people intermittently using the track—and the children, who arrive with granny in the lead, and then take over the park. They particularly enjoy the sculptures, like the reclining bulls they can climb on. (It's a short fall to the grass, which seems to delight them.) This same sequence takes place all over Shanghai every morning, no different than what I've observed in San Francisco in Huntington Park on Nob Hill and Washington Square Park in North Beach.

There is a small coffee and snack shop tucked under one of the more elaborate canopied, wooded sculptures. It's a treat to sit out on the veranda, sipping a coffee and watching the passing parade, which is especially active during holidays or seasonal blooms.

In Jing'An Sculpture Park every plant, bloom, and living thing seems to get personal attention; in China there are hordes of caretakers changing plots of flowers constantly, mowing the lawns, and keeping the park pristine. You almost never see one person doing a task alone, except for sweeping. Typically five or six are at any task and of course there is also an array of "guards" who stroll around in their often ill-fitting, gray, military-style uniforms.

Uniforms are seen everywhere, on doormen, garage attendants, and various order keepers, including those scattered in housing complexes. A brimmed cap is de rigueur. None of them actually have police powers, but they appear as if they do. We would call them security guards. The official look of the uniforms is belied by the fact that they are often rumpled and two sizes too big or too small. Some of the uniformed wear red armbands but oddly not slid up the sleeve, but rather pinned on and hanging off the sleeve.

One day I witnessed a confrontation between a park guard and a young father that could be heard for blocks. The park guards blow their whistles if they think you are tramping in an area that you shouldn't. This includes all of the grass. The shrill, annoying whistles punish everyone, even those who aren't violating the rules. When they are not blowing the whistles, they're yelling at children, mostly for behaving like children. The father in question responded after his child was chastised by a guard. He reprimanded the guard in no uncertain terms. This, in turn, created a shouting match that went on and on as father and guard crossed the park.

These kinds of confrontations are infrequent, but not speaking Chinese, I'm never sure if they are angry and loud or just loud. Any confrontation immediately gathers a crowd. It's incredibly easy to draw a crowd in Shanghai since there are people everywhere. At times I've seen members of a gathered crowd inject themselves into the fray. That triggers others to join in. It's almost like watching a public sport, although there is rarely a clear winner, and eventually the crowd seems to get bored and then drifts away.

However, sometimes the crowd turns dangerous and nasty if the responsible person is acting in an unsympathetic manner. This is especially true in traffic accidents where a small child or woman is hurt. Woe betide the foreigner involved in this kind of accident. When I worked in Jakarta, Indonesia, the standard instruction regarding traffic accidents was "don't stop, no matter what you have done." The reason given was that crowds would immediately form and take the law into their own hands. The rule was, get out of there, find the nearest police station, and report the accident to them.

I once observed a very smug European lounging on one of the low walls reading a book. A guard told him to get off the wall. A tug of war began in two languages. The European refused to move and the guard refused to give up telling him to. I was embarrassed for the guard. No doubt he was following some instruction, silly as it may have been. I was tempted to go tell the foreigner to be courteous, respect the guard, and as a visitor just do what he was asked, but I thought that he looked like the kind of person who wouldn't. I walked on, enjoying the sculpture if not the peace.

Some visitors don't respect the environment in China. There was an incident caught on cell phones and posted on the Internet earlier this year of a European sitting in a crowded train. He put his smelly, bare feet on the headrest of the person in front of him. The lady politely asked that he take them down, telling him they smelled. He mocked her and refused. She tried over and over and he got more and more abusive. Multiple people got into the act and he was intransigent and more and more rude. This went viral online and he was quickly identified as a string player in the Beijing orchestra. He lost his job. I hoped he'd been kicked out of the country.

Incidents like that one tend to cause little explosions of antiforeigner sentiments, but they don't seem to last unless there are several incidents in a row. The more egregious the conduct the greater the reaction is—especially if the conduct includes a Chinese girl and a Caucasian guy.

There are limits on accessibility to some international websites (like YouTube; the Chinese have their own version, YouKu); there are multiple, well-visited sites like China Smack (www.chinasmack.com) that focus on scandals like the man with the smelly feet, as well as car wrecks, scantily clad coeds, outrageous public behavior, and government bureaucrats acting arbitrarily. There's some enthusiasm in exposing faked photos in which public officials are supposedly inspecting a site when they were never there. It's just Photoshopped.

But Shanghai is mostly free of bad public behavior, including in its many parks—some covering acres, others what we call "vest pocket" parks, little kerchiefs of green tucked into a block or along a small road. I'd be less likely to see that rude European in a park than I would a granny with a child bearing one of the brightly colored balloons sold at the entrance or a bride posing for her portrait. Parks are often used for wedding photography, which usually features the lovely settings, especially during bloom times. The young brides appear in full white dress, with their grooms being dragged along, accompanied by three or four people from the professional photography studios. Usually the man is not yet her husband; wedding photos are done well in advance of the event. From observing many wedding photo shoots, this seems to be quite a daunting task for the soon-to-be-wed couple. They endure many poses, hair adjustments, shifting angles, and not many off-camera smiles.

If the park as backdrop doesn't please the bride and her handlers, there are a few extremely popular streets in the old French Concession that get loads of activity. The draw is the old buildings whose façades haven't been changed since the early 1900s, miraculously saved by local wise men who didn't want to see the whole city flattened for high-rises. These buildings were mainly inhabited by foreigners until 1941 and after 1949, by multiple local families. As wealth increased, they reverted again to single families, corporations and government officials who are allowed to move into some of the homes. They refurbish the inside and keep the outsides as they were as part of the deal.

If all else fails for the bridal party, there is always the movie set. Ang Lee's 1930s recreation of old Shanghai for *Lust, Caution*, famously censored because of the steamy sex scenes, is here. The movie was based on local Eileen Chang's short story, who is said to have had a very racy existence herself. Some of the set for Lee's elegant, atmospheric movie is still standing in a studio and photographers flock there to recreate scenes from prewar Shanghai. These photography studios also do setups for "glam" photos, where young women dress up in various snazzy outfits with appropriate backdrops.

Some of the larger parks charge admission but Jing'An Sculpture Park is not one of them. It is gated at night, probably because they don't want vandalism or people falling into the ponds. As a senior citizen I am exempt from charges not only in the parks but almost everywhere (although one of the benefits has been preempted by the Chinese government recently having made all museums free). Since I am a good boy and never violate the terms of my visa I get to enjoy the parks free. Meanwhile Jing'An Sculpture Park is in its daily rhythm and I'm glad to be a neighbor.

I often tell visitors that they ought to visit the parks and one of them, artist Ruth Eckland from the San Francisco area, visited Fuxing Park and wrote this to me about her experience: "People were practicing an ancient form of calligraphy with wet brushes on the pavement; a couple were dancing some wonderful folk dance with recorded music; many families were playing badminton without the need for nets; old tai chi practitioners flowed in quiet nooks; and two men with amazing voices were singing along to recorded opera."

**9.** You may wonder why I put the Chinese characters after names. It is because people are known by the characters, not our Westernized spelling. While I'm at it, my Chinese name is Mi Shu Tai (米书泰). 米 (Mi, rice) suggests abundance, success. 书 (Shu) means wisdom or knowledge, book or writer. 泰 (Tai) has several meanings, including a life of safety and affluence. Tai Mountain ranks top among China's famous mountains, and it means the best. Mountain also means the personality of maturity and kindness, as well as long life. Of course I then climbed Mt. Tai to confirm all this. 书泰 means the determined will to be the best and to solve tough problems. All very flattering because my name was created by some students and over many months argued over every single *hànzì* and settled on these. I was very touched to be presented with a lovely chop and red ink pad when they officially named me.

# Chapter 9

## *Changing Seasons, Changing Clothes*

As seasons change they call for a full makeover of bedclothes and personal apparel. I haven't had to have so many different set of clothes since my student days in New York and working in Washington, DC. I had forgotten how much of a ritual is involved in putting the heavy comforters away and packing heavy sweaters, gloves, and scarves onto high shelves. Away go the multiple heaters, and the air conditioning gets set to cool.

They call it the Plum Rain season.[10] A cloud moves slowly toward the building. First you hear the rumble of thunder and brief flashes in the sky, and then it gets darker and darker. Soon the building's outside lights go on and the rain begins, then comes a torrent as the lightning and thunder produce their display. Looking at the adjacent buildings, the interior lights become visible as do one's neighbors in their apartments eating, sitting, and walking around. It is just like night but in the afternoon.

Summer is when the girls do two intriguing things. They start wearing lots less clothing and many pastel umbrellas sprout up. Ladies here like to stay as pale as they can, which I'm told is seen as a sign of real beauty (true through much of Asia). Many of the old-time posters of qi pao ladies in the 1920s of Shanghai are shown with very pale skin. This somewhat slinky outfit is called cheongsam, in Cantonese dialect most often heard in San Francisco.

Being from foggy San Francisco, I find girls in very lightweight outfits very unusual; for those strutting up Nanjing Xi Lu or Huaihai Lu, it is quite pleasant. Men in my office in Singapore would remark about the unending stream of lightly clad damsels being lifted by the escalators to be presented onto the square step after escalating step. A visual treat.

Schools are out most of the summer so there are no more horns honking in the morning with mothers delivering their children to the local school and no more National Anthem played at 8:10 a.m. Red scarves are put away until the end of summer.

Later in the summer, especially in late July and the first weeks of August, you can hear the din of the cicada in the trees lining the streets. They seem to get started later in the day, so the morning music, much more melodious, is of the birds who happily sing to each other.

There are various festivals and special summer programs in Shanghai, just as there are in most places. One of the nice things about where I live is that from time to time the local committee puts on some kind of event. We had an outdoor movie that reminded me of old black-and-white movies in which soldiers at the front would be watching a film on a bedsheet. Everyone gathers in an open space with plastic chairs and mats arranged as dusk settles in and an old movie projectors starts, its large film reel clickety-clacking as it feeds through the old-fashioned machine, and the show is on.

Kids squiggle around and often bound into the dark, some people chat with their neighbors, and others watch intently. There is something very comforting about an outdoor, casual, communal movie. People come and go, stand, and sit surrounded by twenty-four-story buildings hovering far above the bushes and trees.

Actually, the open-air movies aren't out of character for this country; a lot of life in China is presented in public. Many people sit around along the streets chatting, with their light folding chairs or small tables. They may eat dinner with a few friends right on the sidewalk paying no attention to the passing parade. Laundry is hung for all to see, a T-shirt or mama's underwear. No problem.

Kids play on the sidewalk, couples hold hands, shops open and close. The local evening dance group practices just next to another group swinging to a different tune. People exercise totally unself-consciously right in the sidewalk traffic flow. A wrinkled and worn man holds his cigarette by his thumb and index finger as he reads the morning paper in the sunshine oblivious to others. What must he have seen over the years of turmoil that have swept through Shanghai?

Each summer I spend July in San Francisco. I do it for several reasons, one of which is to flee the oppressive heat. The other is that a club I belong to meets for a few weeks each July. A good friend from Texas, Jeff Wentworth, and I spend a week enjoying the company of friendship, the music, art, painting, and talks and wonderful outdoor breakfasts with enticingly warm coffee cake.

Summers as a child were always spent at Lake Tahoe at our home on the Nevada side, in Glenbrook. We kept the same house for almost fifty years, and there I grew from a small child to a teenager to an adult. Going from city life to country living each summer was just how things were for us. Very normal. The household would pack up early in June as soon as school ended and within a few days be up at Tahoe. It is a place of memories, and many of my siblings and I still return, even though our home is long gone.

This is where I learned to ride horses and would go on breakfast rides, capped by a breakfast prepared by the lead cowboy, Jack Morgan. His scrambled eggs and pancakes were like nothing you ever tasted before. Sometimes this would be a prelude to a cattle roundup to bring the hundreds of unruly animals to a distant corral. You learned very quickly from the cowboys that you didn't actually run cattle; you walked them. Running them would take weight off them and since they were valued by weight you had to coax them in the right direction with your horse or a cattle prod, which we called a hotshot. This is a devious device that is about twelve inches long and filled with several batteries. At the tip are two prongs. When you touch cattle with it and push the button an electrical jolt will get them moving in the right direction. Of course being teenagers we had to surreptitiously try it on our friends, bringing great whoops and hollers and vows of retaliation.

The back of our house faced the lake. From our beach we often walked tentatively into the chilly waters of Lake Tahoe. We learned to swim well, dive for golf balls accidentally—or intentionally—hit into the lake and trap crayfish, the tiny, freshwater creatures yielding portions of lobsterlike meat. In our family, the fisherman was my younger brother Jock. He knew how to do it and would, like a good fisherman, not quite tell us his tricks or favorite spots. When he died, quite suddenly in his forties, it was right in our living room as he was getting ready for the next day's fishing.

In summers you learned how to play golf and even once in a while played with your Mom, who though she was horrendous at it, was always amused by her own terrible style. Sometimes you went out to the course at dusk and took practice shots as Mr. Beason the groundskeeper set the sprinklers in the distance. Floyd the golf pro showed you how to stroke the ball with ease. "Not with ferocity," he'd say. You thrilled on that late afternoon when the course was quite deserted and the movie actress Rita Hayworth hit her ball close by and waved.

It was a place for growing up, meeting girls, and having a first girlfriend. For me that was Caroline. Dad came up from the city every few weekends. Our life was spent mostly outdoors, which made it ideal for our parents. From the living room or their room upstairs they could see not only miles across the lake into California but the whole beach and in the other direction, the front lawn. They could easily keep track of what mischief we were all up to.

Many childhood friendships were cemented in the summer as other San Francisco families came up and stayed at the nearby Glenbrook Inn & Ranch. It was a healthy outdoor existence with swimming and running around every day. Tahoe was where my siblings and I learned to drive, thankfully on empty dirt roads. You learned the skills of water skiing, horseback riding, and the lesser-known business of hunting porcupines at night, far up in trees, despite their bulk.

From time to time Bushki or one of our other dogs would have a scrape with a "porky" and come out much the worse for the encounter. The poor dog's face and mouth would be filled with quills and the only way to get them out was go to the veterinarian and knock the dog out with anesthetics and then remove them. A very sad sight when it happened—even after recovery the dog would be licking and moving his jaw to get rid of the aftereffects.

Porcupine quills have a sharp end that you see on their back but a much more insidious hooked portion on the other end which digs in and prevents an easy removal. We always assumed that one encounter would be enough to keep the dogs away, but sadly it was not. Contrary to popular belief, porcupines cannot shoot their quills from their body. The only way they connect is if you actually engage them and with contact they easily attach themselves. We didn't hunt them for sport, but because they would climb to the top of the pine trees and eat the very tips of the new growth, which would eventually kill the tree.

Since Lake Tahoe is over a mile above sea level and there aren't many close cities, the night air is crisp and clear and the sky luminescent. There are millions of stars to see. One night my youngest brother Bill, at dusk, asked me to go lie on the beach and wait for the stars to come out so we could count them. He was about five, I would have been about eighteen. With night approaching we lay on the beach and waited for the first star to appear, and indeed it did before the night sky had established itself. "One" we said. And soon another, "Two." Then a few more as it got darker and darker. We kept the count but only for a while and then were lost in the display of the night sky, Milky Way and all. I don't know what we learned from trying, but somehow it seemed good to have tried.

As we grew older and had our own families, although much smaller, each family would tend to spend time at Glenbrook with its own brood. Only occasionally would multiple families try to stay at the same time. It may be hard to believe, but the house and little adjacent house would sleep about twenty-four without resorting to couches and sleeping bags, which some took to the beach to have an outdoor night adventure.

One time a bunch of the nieces and nephews decided to use our mostly unused ice-cream maker and produce some homemade ice cream. It was an old-fashioned, crank-operated device and ended up making the most delicious ice cream. I loved it.

All of us eventually had our favorite time to stay at the house and mine turned out to be in late September or early October when most of the neighbors and all the summer visitors left the area. It would be so quiet at night you wondered if the world had ended. I loved it because of the solitude, and the lake seemed at that time of year to be very placid. I would read, paint, take walks where, like Thomas Jefferson, I'd sketch and take notes in a small book. I tried to record some of the plants in China Gardens, an area in a box canyon about a mile away.

This canyon was called China Gardens, possibly because there were many immigrant Chinese workers on the railroads in the 1800s. This train spur had passed by our home and through a series of switchbacks, which eventually led into the summit above the Carson Valley, where logs were off-loaded and sent down a flume into the Carson Valley. There they would be picked up by mule or horse teams or put on the trains of the Virginia & Truckee and sent into the heart of the mining area in Virginia City to shore up the mine walls. This was in the heyday of the Nevada gold and silver strikes of the late 1850s.

This whole area of western Nevada, where Lake Tahoe lies, with miles of sagebrush set among astonishingly beautiful mountains, has a rich history of mining, railroads, and fights between Native Americans and settlers. Glenbrook is very dear to our whole family. Two of my brothers died there, my sister still owns a home close by, and several nephews have their own homes in Glenbrook. One of my nieces lives with her husband at Tahoe year-round. Family gatherings when they occur are now held at two nephews' shared home not far from where we and they grew up in the summers.

After spending the summer at Glenbrook we always came back on Labor Day, during the first week in September when school would shortly begin. When we returned Mom would go on a replacement shopping spree to a local store on Clement Street where a relative of ours of indeterminate relationship sold clothes. Since we all sprouted sometimes a few inches in the summer our wardrobe had to be replenished in new school uniforms and everyday clothes. In China, where many families are only one child, they would be astonished to see the amount of clothing it took to take care of six children from San Francisco. Even as much as I love Shanghai it is easy to understand the attraction I have for returning to San Francisco each July.

☙ ☙ ☙

Pretty soon it is all heaters on. The winter is bitter cold in Shanghai. It is a chill that no one can seem to dispel no matter how heated your house or condo. My place has a central system and each room has additional systems to bring heat right into the room. It is not enough; I need two floor heaters and a tall one that swings back and forth as supplements.

What a contrast from my seven years in Singapore, where every day is sunny, albeit with a quick torrential rainstorm in various parts of the island. To say the rain has the power of a fire hose is not an exaggeration. When I first arrived in Singapore I asked a friend where you could get an umbrella that could withstand such downpours. He said, "a coffee shop, and by the time you are finished the streets will be dry." He was so right even to the dryness of the streets. That's what being on the equator does. You have to let the warm equatorial weather be a joyful part of your daily life and not resent it as some visitors do. But it's much harder not to resent the Shanghai winters.

Even friends who have heated floors and just as modern building as my own are faced with the same nearly insurmountable problem of getting warm in winter. What we all eventually do is sit next to the portable heater.

At night there is a pile of covers and even then from time to time you shiver. What must people who don't have good heating systems do?

Maybe they sleep in their overcoats.

If you look at the weather reports from elsewhere the temperature seems about the same as here, nevertheless a 5°C or below in Shanghai somehow has a bone-chill factor all its own. And I say that having lived on the East Coast of the United States and visited some truly cold cities like Minneapolis in the winter. I was taught years ago in New Hampshire to wrap a scarf across my mouth so the air would be cooled before it hit your lungs. If you didn't you would get lung burn, which could really hurt. To not have a car key stick inside the lock—back in the day before everyone had electronic keys—people used to carry around some kind of squirt device that they squirt into the lock just prior to the key going in; otherwise it would be gripped by the cold and unable to be removed. That must be a lost art today.

In Alaska I was shown how to open a car door without letting the skin of your hand touch it (otherwise it would stick). An old child's trick is to have someone stick their tongue to a steel utility pole and of course then you can't get unstuck until someone warms the spot. In Alaska they have a cord drooping out of the front of the car like an abandoned umbilical cord—an electrical cord attached to a heater that is plugged in at night to keep the engine block warm. If you don't then it will crack from the cold.

So aren't all these places colder than Shanghai? No doubt but somehow, even compared to a racing wind off the Hudson River at night, Shanghai takes the cake.

One way to beat the cold is to run away, which is exactly what I do every December. I go to San Francisco and have a Christmas tree, "midnight" Mass (at 8 p.m. if possible), dinner with Ann Miller and any visiting relatives and friends. Christmas also meant going to the home of my mother's closest friend, Suzie Jane Guittard (who passed away a few years ago) for a Christmas Eve party that included the same buffet every year. This is in the same house where, from the time of my infancy, I used to play with my contemporary Hoddy, one of her three sons.

One of the quirks of the party was there were never any invitations or any announcement at all. You just went and found the same people gathered, throughout the years. Some were born into the party as we grew up and had families, and of course some disappeared in the normal life span. I'm sure I went for at least sixty years. It all started when we lived next door in the late 1930s or '40s. Mom and Dad and their two, then three, then four, until then we had to move because the place wasn't big enough. But we only moved six blocks down Jackson Street to Walnut. Two more boys arrived there.

I have some very vivid memories of living at 3879 Jackson Street. I was born there and we stayed until I was about eight. My brother throwing my glasses out the window. Emma rocking my bed so I fell asleep after scoffing at her that it wouldn't do anything but hurt the springs, only to fall dead asleep within minutes. I distinctly remember standing in our kitchen as the announcement of the bombing of Pearl Harbor came on the radio, and I could see the concerned looks of my parents but didn't understand what was going on. I asked my father what was the matter but he tried to assure me that it was nothing. I instinctively knew that it wasn't true but had no sense of anything other than a tense concern from them.

Dad became an air-raid warden and had a white helmet like those you see on World War I soldiers, with a triangular logo in the front. His job when the sirens went off was to go outside and make sure all the neighbors and cars passing turned off their lights. We would proceed to the basement and huddle together, Mom, my sister and brother and me. We had sand buckets in case a bomb hit and we had to put out a fire. Shades were black and lights off, but there must have been candles because I can still see Mom sitting with all of us close by. Later the sirens would wail again and you could go back upstairs.

Many years later I told this story to a Japanese friend who was my contemporary.

"Yes," he said. "I had the same childhood experience, but the bombs dropped." He was from Tokyo.

Being a child is an adventure in not only discovering the people and world around you but your own abilities. I don't know why I remember it but when I was probably three I was taking a bath and was examining my penis and could see the "inside" and it looked like blood was there. When I got out I asked my mother why the blood didn't come out. I forget what she said, which no doubt satisfied me but I do remember my sister standing by with a smirky laugh as if she knew. She was all of eight. I thought it was a very logical question. "Piss" came out, so why didn't blood? Maybe I should have been a doctor.

I was curious when my Mom was pregnant with my next brother Jock, and one day left for the hospital and then came back with Jock!

Now how did that work? I asked Mom how he got out and she vaguely pointed her side but being a bright little boy I wanted to see. The diversions began and I lost interest. Needless to say I found out much later (but earlier than my dear parents anticipated) from a friend's father's medical books.

One of the things you did during the war was plant a Victory Garden. In our backyard we planted various things, including radishes, and in the middle the plants were arranged in the Morse code pattern of V: dot, dot, dash meaning victory.

Dad was in the coast guard in San Francisco Bay because he was too old to serve and had too many kids. The family would go down to the Marina Greens next to the bay and wave to him as his little cutter came by. The concept was that the coast guard would spot any submarines trying to sneak in the bay. There was a net stretched across the Golden Gate Bridge's base to prevent this but when it was lowered for a ship to pass there was the possibility of a sub going directly underneath at the same time. No one ever told the Japanese this so we were free from subs and Dad and his band of makeshift coast guardsmen spent most of their time shooting at stray seals (they called that "target practice") and getting extra rations to bring home from the ship. Since every family had ration books with coupons for various staples this haul from the boat brought great joy to the household.

One of the good friends he made on the ship was a captain in the San Francisco fire department, "Uncle Ben," who would come over to the house from time to time and let us ride in the chief's car, and he would very briefly blow the siren to our absolute delight. He even let us visit the fire station and sit on the hook-and-ladder truck and slide down the fire pole.

The day the war ended Emma took me to Sacramento Street where a great celebration had spontaneously broken out and someone was banging on a utility pole with a hammer—making a great din—where a cheering and clapping crowd had gathered. I noticed a cheering person that, from my five-year-old perspective, was an enemy since he looked Japanese. I couldn't understand why he was cheering if "they" had lost. What Emma said is now vague, but no doubt the enthusiast was Chinese since sadly, all the Japanese Americans had been shipped off to prison camps. This blot in our history was only formally erased years later when President Ronald Reagan apologized in a separate letter and issued compensation to everyone still living who had suffered that indignity. My secretary at the time, Rose Kimura, received one of the letters. Ironically, at the end of the war the American army unit with the greatest number of combat citations was the one made up of Japanese Americans, the famous 442nd.[11]

Both my uncles were in the service: my uncle Russ in the China/Burma theater and my uncle John in the Pacific in the navy. I still have some of their unit patches and medals.

The winter of life seems to bring the gusher of childhood memories, both of lessons learned and small hardships faced, like when my brother threw my glasses out the window, only found later unbroken in the garden during the subsequent hunt with Emma. I was grumpy then because he was not properly punished for this infraction, but more often, I was in league with him, say, when we were learning that you could stand on the sink in our bedroom and piss in it without being discovered. In that very room Emma rocked me to sleep when I resisted my mandatory pre-school afternoon nap. Looking at my sister's dollhouse when she wasn't around and wondering what the attraction was. Scraping my knees playing because we wore short pants, throwing dirt clods at the other neighborhood kids, one of whom turned out many years later to be the founder of the GAP. Getting in trouble with some other little boys because we told a younger neighbor girl that if she jumped on a certain spot of dirt in the garden a fairy castle would appear, only to have her little dress splashed with mud as she pounced on the middle water mudhole we had deviously prepared, covered with paper sprinkled with dirt. We ran.

We used to line up on the couch listening to my mother read Ernie Pyle's column in the evening newspaper as he told the stories of men in the war. I was nicknamed "Clip" by my grandfather after telling him the long story of the Pan Am Clipper as we watched one take off from the bay from his upstairs study.

We attended our one and only Passover meal with the lovely Jewish couple Cantor Rinder and his wife, who lived in the lower flat before we moved. He was the cantor in the local Jewish synagogue, Temple Emanu-El, and took these wiggly, scrawny Irish children to the temple and showed us the beauty and holiness of the place. Periodically his wife would call upstairs and ask my mom to have the children (then three of us) to stop running around. My eight- or nine-year-old sister used to cry uncontrollably when my parents would go out to dinner for the evening. She would hide in the living room closet and cry and cry. I suppose today's parents would seek some psychological help, a learned text, or pills to "cure" her, but in those days my savvy parents just let her grow out of it, which she shortly did. Then there was the time I was reprimanded for my bringing a snake home in my pocket and deviously pulling it out during a tea party my mom was having. I knew it would get a reaction and indeed it did. I later kept my pet snake in a large cardboard box in my best friend John Mason's garden and fed it odd bits I got from some pet store. It didn't last long.

Maybe this tangent into my life in San Francisco, the city where summer is colder than winter and neither are particularly so, represents my desire to avoid even thinking about winter in Shanghai. But I'll go back to it in words because it represents such a significant part of my life now.

One nice thing about winter—there have to be a few, right?—is that you get to see where the birds build their nests. This is especially clear on the long road from the Beijing airport into the central business district. There are long lines of trees roadside that go on for miles, and during the winter these trees lose all their leaves and expose the multiple bird nests in almost every tree, a glimpse into secret lives. And there are of course the occasional snow falls. These come quite infrequently to Shanghai and when it happens it quiets the whole city, spreading the calm of snow to an otherwise hectic pace. The first snowfall is always the best, covering the cityscape with a completely new look. Walking along the usual routes feels like going to new places. The snow usually lasts a day and then melts away.

Then there are the New Year's celebrations, which bring a din of firecracker explosions such as I'd never heard before. This takes place on the last night of the lunar calendar at midnight and goes on and on and on. It then repeats five days later when the god of fortune is welcomed. Firecrackers in long, noisy strings; bottle rockets; exploding, large, sky-brightening fireworks—just when you think the last person has run out, it begins again. I can look out my window and have an unobstructed view for miles, and it is like seeing some kind of war scene with flashes and explosions taking place in all directions, near and far. It is beautiful in some respects but the cacophony is deafening even when you are indoors. Each family apparently sends off a few just as part of their ritual.

Tangyuan is part of the New Year family-gathering ritual. It is a rice ball whose main ingredient is glutinous rice flour and often has a core of either peanut, bean, or sesame depending upon taste and what part of the country you come from. The balls, along with boiling water, are placed in bowls and eaten together with the family members. The ball symbolizes family harmony.

It is interesting when you talk to educated people about various rituals and folk beliefs and their own beliefs. One very educated young woman who works for an international company and has traveled extensively one day told me she couldn't come to dinner because she had to stay at home that day and night. Why? It was the day the ghosts of your ancestors came around and food was put out for them, and you weren't allowed to leave home or something awful might befall you. I asked her if she really believed this and she said no. And then "but." In other words she was just covering her bets. Tradition and ancient beliefs are wrapped into annual rituals where a certain behavior is expected even though deep down you don't believe it.

Looking back on my time in Singapore, all high-tech and wired, you might imagine it would be a place where most would ignore such "old wives' tales." No way. During Hungry Ghost two days, when the spirits of ancestors are supposed to come back and hang around, all over town tables of food are placed in front of business establishments, "money" is burned on the street, and in the financial district you walk by little piles of burnt ashes or small ashtray-sized flower arrangements, a burned incense stick, and food arrangements. Do people walking by this into their skyscrapers believe the ghosts are around? Likely no, but no harm; it's just in case.

One New Year I had the privilege of joining with my friend Joanna Way and her family for the traditional New Year's dinner. Her parents, daughter, and her husband's relatives were all seated at one large table in a huge restaurant. Many of these family events are held in public restaurants that are fully booked well in advance. Each table is beautifully appointed with dishes and utensils and an unending flow of food until finally there is not room enough for all the dishes and the guests. Table after table has young and old gathered, all laughing and talking and eating and drinking. It is quite festive and many photos are taken. Later you return to their home and still more food is presented, Joanna's daughter Silvia gave us a presentation of her lovely ballet technique and we adjourned again to light sparklers and firecrackers with neighbors.

The same kind of thing is happening all over China from the bright lights of Shanghai, Hong Kong, and Beijing to the little hidden valleys and villages in Heilongjiang, Xinjiang, Fujian, or Yunnan. A billion people in family ritual.

10. The season of the Plum Rains or intermittent drizzle, is a special meteorological phenomenon of the middle and lowland areas of the Yangtze River. Usually, the Plum Rain season starts in the middle of June and ends in early July, lasting for about twenty days. *Shanghai Times*

11. The 442nd Regimental Combat Team of the United States Army was composed of enlisted Japanese American men. They fought primarily in Europe. The families of many of its soldiers were subject to internment. The 442nd was a self-sufficient force and fought with uncommon distinction. The unit became the most highly decorated regiment in the history of the United States Armed Forces, including twenty-two medal of honor recipients. The motto of the 442nd Regimental Combat Team was "go for broke."

## Chapter 10

## *Spirit of Enterprise*

When I went to Shanghai to start Spirit of Enterprise, I wasn't exactly a novice at attempting to bring the concept of entrepreneurship to a Communist country. In 2005, I set up an office for Spirit of Enterprise in Vietnam. It was not what you might expect when doing the same thing in Singapore or San Francisco. Nothing is quite straightforward. This is in harmony with the disharmony in the government's split personality on communism and capitalism. You can't get a licensee as a nonprofit unless you are a part of a government organization, but that is not easy. You can incorporate as a regular company, which is what we opted for, while running it as a nonprofit. We did the same thing later in China.

Vietnam is still driven by its formative Communist ideology. Although they are smart enough to recognize that doesn't make good economics, they aren't ready to leap into capitalism like China. At least not yet. Hence the businesses operate in this "no man's land" of conflicting laws and aspirations and tend not to value extra education probably because the very entrepreneurs who created the businesses didn't have much education, just a lot of guts and savvy.

One of the original SOE board members from Singapore had an office in Vietnam and helped get things going for us in Hanoi.[12] In Vietnam, when you rent an office, your business name may not fit what you are doing, but this doesn't seem to bother anyone. Even our landlord lacked a business incorporated for renting space in the building, also a four-story walk-up, maybe once a house (like many of the surprisingly clean $25-a-night hotels where I stayed). I couldn't even be certain she actually owned the building, because we don't pay rent to anyone but her and always in cash. We didn't declare it and neither did she. She may have just had some kind of lease on our quarters. Or maybe not. The convoluted system also worked for the office phones. I never got it quite clear who actually was leasing the lines to us—maybe they were just hijacked off someone else's line—but every so often some guy would come into the office, purporting to be the telephone company, and collect our monthly charges. Of course no receipt was offered or needed. Taxes, accounting business reports? Forget it. Cash in and cash out. As you can imagine, at first this really bothered me. But then I got used to how things worked.

When I first brought Spirit of Enterprise to Shanghai I was also lucky enough to get help from one of my former Singapore board members, K. H. John Chong, who had been transferred to Shanghai. He became a real cheerleader for me as I began the process of settling in and starting up. My first focus was on getting some staff in place. One of the first hires was Vivian Li, Li Mai Lei (李迈雷), whom I have mentioned above as my savior in getting my banking and other tasks done. Vivian turned out to be my Chinese counterpart of Kelly Teoh in Singapore, with all the same great qualities, including never giving up.

About once a week I would meet with my staff and we planned the next week and solved current problems. Everyone, including me, got a list of "to dos." We'd meet at 41 Hengshan Lu, where I had a serviced apartment. The library there was quite nice and quiet and a pleasant place to have a meeting, and then the team would go to whatever makeshift office we had found to operate from. We were "hermit crabs," living in these borrowed spaces. And my small staff was spoiled by living in others' offices, including the good people from the Singapore government and later in the office of my good friends Jenny and Bob Theleen. The Theleens let us camp in their ChinaVest office on the Bund and were generous to make us a gift of the office facilities, equipment, and even their board room. The office had sweeping views of Pudong, and it was especially intriguing as dusk settled into night and the remarkable illuminated sides of the buildings became live television advertisements. Even better than the setting was the fact that Jenny agreed to become our board chair.

☙ ☙ ☙

Having the right people, either board members or staff, is crucial of course. In Vietnam I'd struggled to find good staff for the office. We needed people who could work on their own and were self-starters. It caused constant voluntary turnover as the people would often be adrift without specific day-to-day direction. Some of this can be laid at the doorstep of a country in transition. You can't go from rice farmer to self-starting entrepreneur in a few generations and expect no difficulties. I was lucky to find a superior executive director, Nguyen Phuong Lan, whose background can give you a sense of what some of these talented people go through to get the education they want. Lan, like many others, came from a very humble background. She lived with her family and worked all day and into the evening for a computer company. In her "free time" she would volunteer to direct our employees and make sure Spirit of Enterprise Vietnam was on the right track.

Sometimes she did so quite literally. I remember one day when I had my arms firmly wrapped around Lan's waist, her motorbike careening ahead into a four-way intersection where hundreds of other motorbikes were heading at the same time but from four different directions. How can this work? No signals, everyone heading in their own direction. Is it possible to get through? I can attest that it is. It is a combination of "chicken," skill, courtesy, experience, and especially catching the flow as different directions deftly yield and proceed. Those of a libertarian bent would revel in it. This was even before the pre-helmet requirement days. Easy riders every one.

Young men would ogle and flirt with not unwilling girls at very close range, families would cluster with three or more on one bike. When you are riding right next to someone in traffic it is hard to be unpleasant, so people seem more courteous, almost as if they are pedestrians having a bit of fun. I found it most charming to see girls in their traditional pastel *ao dai* outfits and *nón lá* (leaf hats), holding umbrellas and feigning oblivion to the cute boys passing smiles. Some say the ao dai covers everything, but hides nothing—similar, I would say to the Chinese *qi pao*.

The conical head covering is worn by young and old, city slickers, and most farm people all over Asia. It is perfect for keeping the sun off and for the young women on their bikes, it provides shade along with their long gloves and face masks. All for protection against the sun. They don't want to let their skin lose its whiteness.

Gradually, over the four years we had a Spirit of Enterprise office in Vietnam, more and more cars came on to the roads. They pretty much stuck to the center lanes, but it was like schools of fish swimming next to a hungry shark. They could hurt you. They didn't give way and you could get killed if you were hit by a car. The joy of the streets began to get a little dangerous. It was still enjoyable in the countryside though. One day I was invited by a group of recent university graduates to go out to the countryside and have a picnic. Great care is taken riding the roads on motorbikes, as you are constantly being overtaken or overtaking old trucks with dubious braking power, but it's fun. And it gave me a chance to see the suburbs, which provide a glimpse of what unfortunately will come to Hanoi. Duplicative three-story homes and cement shopping strips. The homes are tall and skinny because tax is determined by front footage; make your house tall and thin, pay fewer taxes. Why doesn't Notre Dame in Paris have steeples? The same reason—steeples were the tax measure for the whole building; if you didn't have any you didn't get taxed. Interesting how taxes influence design. In Vietnam, for sure!

Without fail I found most Vietnamese quite friendly, especially the university students. I spoke multiple times to the Hanoi School of Business at the University of Vietnam and never once heard anything but admiration for America. It was always a joy to speak to these students and the language was English; the language of business worldwide, although I remember when I was lecturing to Japanese businessmen I often said the language of the world was Arabic numerals. The Hanoi students had to be proficient in English or they could not complete their degree. They asked lots of questions, were funny, quick, and attentive. By the way, the Hanoi School of Business is not funded by the university, i.e., the government, rather by its most successful entrepreneur, the founder of a software company that at one time represented half the value of the Vietnam stock exchange. I might remind the "tisk tisk" head nodders that this is exactly how Stanford University started.

In regular interactions with the Vietnamese, the little matter of the American involvement in the "war of liberation" is never raised. When I would bring it up and try to get some kind of insight, they really offered none or something vague like, "Oh, yes I think my grandfather was in it." Even at the notorious Hanoi Hilton, the prison that held many Americans, you have to go through room after room before Americans are mentioned. From the Vietnamese point of view the Americans just came into the very end of a war of liberation from the French that lasted for decades. It was the French who were the culprits.

My enthusiasm for Spirit of Enterprise Vietnam remains, although when my executive director Lan left for the United States—more on how she did that later—we had to close the office. Hopefully we will begin again when she returns, although she won't be involved as she once was since Coke is sending her to Ho Chi Minh City (Saigon, Sài Gòn), the commercial center of the country (whereas Hanoi is the political and national capital). I am hopeful we can get Spirit of Enterprise going again with the help of Coca-Cola because there is real enthusiasm especially in the south for creating new businesses. I expect this time around it will be a little easier to sustain.

Assembling the board in Shanghai was a bit tough, but gradually we put together a varied group of about fifteen members. One of whom, we found out subsequently, who had been urged on us by our errant staff member, and who was being closely monitored by the internal security services for dissident activities. He turned out not to have been a good fit for us although the issue of any dissident activities never seemed to arise. He was only on the board for about six months. In retrospect, his telling me one day that he was thinking of moving to Hong Kong and would not be able to participate in future board meetings made sense.

Another board member was a woman who was a very creative television producer. She had invented multiple programs, one of which drew more than one hundred million viewers each week. That's not a typo, it really was one hundred million. The CEO of one of the largest insurance companies in China, someone I had known from my investment banking days, also joined the board. I first called on his company in China when I think it had about $20 million in capital, and by the time he joined the board more than fifteen years later the capital was about $2 billion. "You should have invested, Russell," he said one day to me. Right.

We were always on the lookout for both students to interview entrepreneurs and good stories from entrepreneurs. One of the first people I heard about was a young man, Lan Haiwen (兰海文), who had started a game-software company. A friend in the United States who had worked in the largest US game company, Electronic Arts, told me about him and that he was someone who was "up and coming." That turned out to be an understatement.

We got connected and we agreed to meet at the well-worn Jin Jiang Hotel on South MaoMing Lu. This was the very first hotel I had ever stayed in about 1986 and had been the site for visiting foreign leaders; President Nixon, who signed the famous Shanghai Communiqué, which recognized the PRC as the legitimate government of all China, stayed there in 1972.

Lan had a classic story of failure and success. He had started a software game company in 2000 with a couple of friends, and within three years they had fallen out and the company failed. Lan felt that his ideas were solid and in 2005 gathered a few former employees who shared his vision. He had no money to pay them since he was completely wiped out from his previous try, but they agreed to work for a year without pay to try to build something special. And that they did. Today UltiZen Games is the largest all-platform game developer in China. They have more than 450 employees in China and Japan and their games are played worldwide. Recently he has run into some hard times, but I'm sure he will bounce back again.

This whole adventure in gaming gives just a taste of the kinds of thrilling creativity and openness of some of the people I was introduced to through Spirit of Enterprise China. There were many others, but the creation of a new entity isn't all roses. There were plenty of thorns as well. Two of the greatest difficulties were raising money and trying to keep the executive team on the straight and narrow to achieve the board's objectives.

Donations were very slow in coming and we finally worked out a system of benefits for corporate donors. One of the groups was CITIC, one of China's large investment companies. They had an idea about certain kinds of entrepreneurs they were interested in, and SOE did a survey of those companies that had been interviewed that met their criteria. It seemed a satisfactory arrangement. We tried this on multiple companies but in the end there wasn't much forthcoming. A few helpful souls on the board made some efforts but they didn't lead to success. Despite all the glitter and high offices the board was never able to raise any significant funds for paying the upkeep of the staff. If it weren't for Jenny and Bob we wouldn't even have had an office to work from.

Raising money in China is complicated and not intuitive for many potential donors, other than unusually generous people like Lan Haiwen (兰海文). For many it is me first, family second, and no third. In addition the government has a real concern with approving NGOs. Even today, after years of trying to sort things out, it is just now slowly opening the nonprofit sector to slightly easier approvals.

They have a point, most strikingly brought home to me by a minister of women's activities in Cambodia who, in talking about NGOs said, "They are more powerful than we are." She then recounted an incident stimulated by NGOs that caused her to have to fly to Washington, DC, to try to straighten out a matter that had caused Cambodia to be notched down in the US government's categories of aid.

China is very "buttoned up" from an outsider's viewpoint and the Communist Party, and hence the government, doesn't want a lot of outside interference, or criticism, for that matter. NGOs and other nonprofits are always bumping into what governments are expected to do in looking out for the welfare of their citizens. No government, no matter how generous, can do all the things needed. Hence nonprofits and NGOs have a very important role in filling out some of the sectors of help, yet are constantly bumping up against established procedures and minor and major despots.

The problem of donations isn't necessarily personal stinginess. It may also be a combination of Confucian values and government ever-presence. What do I mean?

If the family is the core of society then that is what you should concentrate all your efforts on and use it to enhance and preserve your wealth. Why give to other families, even ones in need? Coupled with that is the ever-presence of the government, which is intertwined in many social and daily activities. "If the government isn't doing it, why should I?" I was told many times in many ways.

If someone is barging into the center of the elevator as the door opens, even though this prevents you from getting out, it is of no concern to those coming in if you don't factor in their construct of the world. This is reinforced somewhat I think by there being no real moral underpinning of a person's actions. There is no overall religion in China, and children aren't brought up to believe in God or any supreme being (when I was a child I'm sure I thought it was a supreme bean and couldn't quite figure out why a bean was so important).

Whether these theories are correct or not, I can say with assurance that slaving in the field of fundraising in China is very, very difficult.

One way to approach the problem was to try to get international companies from the United States to give through organizations that were already tax exempt and then deliver the donation to China. As a member of the advisory council of the Asia Foundation I knew about an organization they had created called Give2Asia, which directed donations and then oversaw their implementation. This worked perfectly for the first year. It required a local Chinese organization approved by Give2Asia to oversee our work. We were under the supervision of the NPO Development Center in Shanghai. This organization was the inspiration of Zhuang Ailing (庄爱玲), a PhD and supreme intellect whose imagination and persistence help new nonprofits get started. By having them help guide our little team, the team was supposed to learn good practices and how to run a nonprofit correctly. Some of the lessons took and some unfortunately didn't.

I had chosen as one of the principal employees a young man from a government organization who had come recommended by one of the officers at the Shanghai Foreign Affairs Office. Everyone on the team worked extraordinarily hard and showed unusual diligence, and under the wing of NPO things went pretty smoothly, or so I thought. What emerged over time was that this young man was unable to take direction from anyone if he didn't agree with it. At the same time, he never voiced a different view. Things just wouldn't get done the way we had expected. It took a long time to have the full problems arise, more than two years, but finally the board got fed up and fired him. All was not negative however because during that time, with others pitching in, we had two books published and multiple students were able to participate. One happy offshoot for me was that several of the young women who had worked hard as volunteers decided to go to the United States for graduate school and I was able to write some very enthusiastic recommendation letters.

After a little more than three years and two books having been published we ran out of money. Well ahead of running out of funds we told the staff to make efforts with our entrepreneur's list, but the young man in the leadership role for some reason wouldn't do anything, including walk to the next building and ask for a renewal investment from CITIC. I never understood his attitude or his intransigence.

We were forced to "temporarily" wind things up. Vivian stoutly took care of all the loose ends so that we didn't have to let go of everything we had built. She arranged to keep the website working with the help of our ever-present tech guru Zhao Xun (赵勋), who continues his magic and has been with us from the very first meeting.

Overall about two hundred students from about twenty universities in three main areas—Shanghai, Beijing, and Hangzhou—participated. About as many entrepreneurs told their stories and hopefully thousands of others listened to the lectures, came to the workshops, went online, or read the books. That's not bad so far and it isn't over yet. We made an arrangement with Shanghai University of Finance and Economics to give some lectures in the now countrywide mandatory course on entrepreneurism to assign the students to do interviews and possibly create an online book of the results.

From the looks of what has transpired in the entrepreneurial field in Shanghai and all over China it is questionable if there is a real need for SOE anymore. It may have fulfilled its mission and can happily withdraw from the field. If you review the number of organizations that focused on entrepreneurs and entrepreneurism over the last ten years since the founding of SOE in Singapore it is remarkable. There are all kinds of organizations and government-backed programs in almost every country today, when there were almost none when we started. I don't believe that organizations have to live forever if their purpose is fulfilled just as well by others, or the main objectives are accomplished. You have to know when to hold 'em and when to fold 'em.

**12.** If you were to look at the Vietnamese words Hanoi should be expressed Hà Nội. This holds true for most of the places; but in English we tend to run the words together.

# Chapter 11

## *We're Keeping an Eye on You*

Because of my decades of work and travel throughout Asia I'm used to unexpected rules.

Take the time I flew into Taipei just for one day just to do a little sightseeing. It was early in the 1980s. Obviously America and Taiwan were very close friends and it never occurred to me that I might need a visa. I arrived about five at night and was going to just look around and leave the next day fairly early. "Where is your visa?" immigration asked me. "I don't have one. Do I need it?" "Please sit over there and we will get back to you." Hours later an officer said I couldn't come into Taiwan and they were confiscating my passport until I was scheduled to leave the next day. I would have to stay in their approved hotel not too far from the airport and would be driven there.

Off we went to a hotel paid for by them. After seeing me registered and telling me not to run around Taipei, they left, saying they would pick me up in the morning. There was no signing in or people watching you—I was on "scout's honor." I could have taken a cab to the tourist hot spots or do anything else I wanted. I didn't because I was tired and a little apprehensive about getting caught leaving the hotel. In the morning they arrived in their minivan, took me to my airport gate, handed me my passport, and wished me a safe journey.

So thirty years later, I am calm in Shanghai when there is a light knock at my door and I open it to find a policeman dressed in plain clothes. He asked something in Chinese and showed me a clipboard with names on it, including my own and my passport number.

I said, "Who are you?" and he said, "Police" and pointed to his credentials hanging from his neck. More for effect (and to stifle the impulse to say "Why should I acknowledge you, buddy? I'm an American") I studied them and when I had finished he said, "Is this your passport number?"

It was and I acknowledged it and, with a little bow of his head, he left.

So what was up? As I already knew and didn't have to read in the booklet available in our lobby titled "Kindly reminding from the Jing'an Police," I had to register my presence at my local police station. This is not unlike when you check into a hotel in many countries and they ask to copy your passport so they can turn it over to the local police. I am diligent in following the rules although I am intrigued by the always-unanswered question "What are you going to do with the information?" Not as a sinister thought but as a bureaucratic one, because so much information, especially tracking, is so duplicative and silly. My whereabouts is gathered in my visa application, my entrance at immigration, my local police box, and my local community committee. Oh yes, it's also gathered in the census. So who needs to know the same stuff four or five times over?

The rule is that each time you come and from China you have to revisit the local police station and give them a form and your passport; then they change the dates on the form and stamp it and return it to you while you wait. The only saving grace is there is often a very cute policewoman who does this and she always flashes a slightly guarded flirt of a smile when she returns my passport and form.

This is only one of the ways that foreigners as well as locals are kept track of. The locals too have to register but only once unless they move. They have their resident identity cards, which everyone carries and there is the Hukou[13] system, instituted by the Communist Party in 1949, which indicates your city of residence.

At our complex as in every living area there is a local committee of semivolunteers who are there to "help out" if you have any problems. Some are paid a tiny stipend and some do it as volunteers. Their photos are posted in our lobby and they drop by periodically to "see that all is well." Since I don't speak Chinese we do our chitchat at the door, which consists merely of indicating I'm the only one living here and that I appreciate them coming by and spying on me. Lots of smiles and friendly demeanor. I wonder if they grill my Ayi about me but I doubt it.

I don't know if anyone bugs my phone calls or not. I sort of doubt that for two reasons, first that not many people really are that comfortable with English. Second, I have my landline disconnected because the only calls I ever received on it were from someone trying to sell something. How do I know? A salesman is very obviously a salesmen in any language.

The guards at our gate are on day and night so they know who visits you, when you come and go. From the looks of them I doubt very much if they are a source of anything too profound other than raising the gate to wave cars in and out.

Even the census people came by last year. They are really efficient. They got me on one try: two ladies, just three or four questions, and then bye, bye. As the United States does, China takes a census every ten years but *they* get the whole thing done in two months. Friends tell me they are absolutely unrelenting in coming back and back if they miss you.

This isn't all benign however. A Shanghainese friend told me about taking some boxes to store for a Western acquaintance who had been a teacher in a local migrant school. About a month later as she was going into her complex she was told by the guard, "Your brother-in-law came by." She has no brother-in-law. She had no doubt that it was Public Security. They had jimmied her door, rifled through the boxes and left but made sure she knew they had been there with the "brother-in-law" message. She was, and still is intimidated. As she related the story her voice quivered. "They can put you in jail for no reason," she said. This is a well-educated woman in her thirties, with a very good government-linked company job. This isn't a story of the past. It is today.

Can you be thrown in jail arbitrarily? Apparently if you cross the wrong guy you can but not as easily as in the past. At Spirit of Enterprise, a Public Security team came and questioned our executive Vivian Li several times.

"They were just boys grinding out some bureaucratic paper-wasting motions," she told me.

We did many things that could raise your head above the berm, from organizing university students to do interviews of entrepreneurs to holding public events with speeches and whoa, having a book published! You can imagine those security teams saying "What are these guys doing?" The second year our guy teamed up with the Communist Party via the China Youth League when having our book published. Maybe that's why none of us were ever further questioned. No worries that the book might have something objectionable in it, however; the publisher is of course government linked and would do its own censoring if needed.

Is arbitrary arrest common? As far as I can tell it is not. What is "out of bounds," as the Singaporeans call it? "You'll find out" is the purposefully vague answer. Of course self-censorship is harsher than any vague rules. That's what they count on.

Want to get a lawyer if you are charged with some kind of wrongdoing, real or imagined? Bo Xilai (薄熙来), the now disgraced former party boss, provided the answer in his heyday. When Bo was appropriating businesses because he coveted their income, one of the leading entrepreneurs whose business was being grabbed was jailed. He got a top lawyer to show how unlawful Bo's actions were. In turn, Bo had the lawyer thrown in jail. The great problem is that when you attain a very high post such as a provincial leader there is almost no countervailing force to stop you from arbitrary actions and grand theft. Except as Bo so forcefully found out; you antagonize some who have higher office and then beware. It reminds me of Coleridge describing Kublai Khan and his enemies: "And all should cry, Beware! Beware! His flashing eyes, his floating hair! Weave a circle round him thrice, And close your eyes with holy dread, For he on honey-dew hath fed, And drunk the milk of Paradise."

As anyone who reads the world press knows, there are many prisoners in China who have landed behind bars for reasons that are easy to understand if you take the view of the Chinese government trying to maintain "harmony." History shows that it is difficult to maintain without a very strong state oversight. How do you maintain harmony with 1.3 billion people in a vast landmass and fifty-five ethnic groups? We would argue that you do it with the consent of the people. But the CCP has never asked the citizen and by its actions is dubious about the possible results. Many of the people I have discussed this with express the wish not to get rid of the CCP but rather to make it open and competitive within the Party itself. The CCP is sort of trying this out in Hong Kong. In the meantime it is tight control and economic growth as the pacifier. However from our point of view some pretty arbitrary things go on fairly regularly.

When the Nobel Peace prize was awarded to Liu Xiaobo (劉曉波), the writer and democracy advocate, you neither read nor heard a word of it in the Chinese press, but when author Mo Yan (莫言) won the Nobel Prize for literature it was all over the media. In one of his most popular novels, *Big Breasts & Wide Hips*, he describes in brutal detail some of the excesses during Mao's tenure. Hence it is very hard to predict black-and-white descriptions of how things work or even what to expect in all cases. Just like any large institution there is lots of tugging and hauling from those representing a variety of views. While some things are off-limits the "limits" are not always the same nor administered in the same manner by a thuggish village chief and the head of the standing committee.

Let me give you a feel for this. Here are a few of the most well-known critics of the government. Some are in jail, some harassed, one escaped.

As just mentioned, Liu Xiaobo: He was jailed in June 2009 on suspicion of "inciting subversion of state power." The winner of the Nobel Peace Prize in 2010 actively participated in the writing of and, along with more than three hundred Chinese citizens, signed Charter '08. The charter is a manifesto released on December 10, 2008, to coincide with the sixtieth anniversary of the adoption of the Universal Declaration of Human Rights. It was written in the style of the Czechoslovak Charter 77, calling for more freedom of expression, human rights, more democratic elections, for privatizing state enterprises and land, and for economic liberalism. The Chinese charter has collected over ten thousand signatures.

Ai Weiwei (艾未未) is a contemporary artist, active in sculpture, installation, architecture, curating, photography, film, and social, political, and cultural criticism. Ai was commissioned as the artistic consultant for design, for the Beijing National Stadium (the Bird's Nest) for the 2008 Summer Olympics. In December 2008, Ai supported an investigation, started by another Chinese artist, into student casualties in the 2008 Sichuan earthquake. Called the "citizen's investigation," it aimed to compile a list of students killed in the earthquake by May 12, 2009, the earthquake's first anniversary.

As of April 14, 2009, the list had accumulated 5,385 names. Ai published the collected names as well as numerous articles documenting the investigation on his blog, which was shut down by Chinese authorities in May 2009. He also posted his list of names of schoolchildren who died on the wall of his office at FAKE Design in Beijing. Ai suffered headaches and claimed he had difficulty concentrating on his work since returning from Chengdu in August 2009, where he was beaten by the police for trying to testify for Tan Zuoren, a fellow investigator of the shoddy construction and student casualties in the earthquake.

In September 2009, Ai was diagnosed to be suffering internal bleeding in a hospital in Munich, Germany, and the doctor arranged for emergency brain surgery. The cerebral hemorrhage is believed to be linked to the police, who detained him when he was beaten. In 2012 he was accused of tax evasion and fined over $2 million, which he protested and took to the courts but lost. Thousands of supporters sent in over $1 million to him, but he is returning it.

Chen Guangcheng (陈光诚) was arrested, jailed, beaten, and escaped to the United States. He is the blind Chinese civil-rights activist who worked on human rights issues in rural areas of China. In 1997, the leaders of Chen's village began implementing a land-use plan that gave authorities control over 60 percent of land, which they then rented out at high cost to the villagers.

The plan, known as the "two-field system," was a major source of enrichment for the local government. While studying in Nanjing the following year, however, Chen learned that the program was illegal, and he petitioned central authorities in Beijing to end the system, thereby irritating local officials.

In March 2004, more than three hundred residents from Chen's village of Dongshigu filed a petition to the village government demanding that they release the village accounts—which hadn't been made public for over ten years—and address the issue of illegal land requisitions. When village authorities failed to respond, villagers escalated their appeals to the township, county, and municipal governments, still without response. Village authorities then began to publicly threaten villagers. In November 2004, Chen acted on behalf of villagers to file a lawsuit in the Qi'nan County Court against the local Public Security Bureau for negligence. The case was accepted, and proceedings began in early 2005.

In 2005, Chen spent several months surveying residents of Shandong province, collecting accounts of forced, late-term abortions and forced sterilization of women who stood in violation of China's one-child policy. His survey was based in Linyi, a city of ten million about four hundred miles southeast of Beijing, and included surrounding rural suburbs. Chen later recalled that his survey would have been significantly larger in scope were he not limited by a lack of financial resources.

Chen gained international recognition for organizing a landmark class-action lawsuit against authorities in Linyi, Shandong, for what was claimed to be excessive enforcement of the one-child policy. As a result of this lawsuit, Chen was placed under house arrest from September 2005 to March 2006, with a formal arrest in June 2006. On August 24, 2006, Chen was sentenced to four years and three months for "damaging property and organizing a mob to disturb traffic." He was released from prison in 2010 after serving his full sentence, but remained under house arrest or "soft detention" at his home in Dongshigu Village. Chen and his wife were reportedly beaten shortly after a human-rights group released a video of their home under intense police surveillance in February 2012. In an escape that was publicized in the West, he got to the American Embassy in Beijing and after lots of wrangling the authorities let him leave China for NYU School of Law.[14]

How paranoid can a government get? Even more. It seemed preposterous as well as bizarre to us, but during the week of the eighteenth CPC National Congress held in 2012 to elect new leadership, the cabs in Beijing were told to lock the electric windows so they could not be opened by a passenger. The reason was "safety" said the authorities. The real reason is that people have used the back window of cabs to throw out flyers as they speed away. The authorities don't want this going on especially not during the National Congress. Furthermore, any passenger who asked a cab driver to go to Tiananmen Square—where the Congress was meeting—had to show their identity card to the driver to be recorded and registered.

All this certainly shows a real sense of insecurity by the CCP. Looking around my city of Shanghai you would tend to be fairly acclimated to the small things such as signing up at the police station, but overall there probably is much more going on than the average person is aware of. Ponder this: China's security apparatus has more people working for it than the Chinese army.

So the government is very diligent in keeping track of everyone, and they are just as diligent in making sure we don't see or hear anything that might undermine social harmony. The Chinese government is paranoid about anything that doesn't follow their line no matter the medium. In the '50s and later it was wall posters anonymously posted in Beijing. Then came the Internet, which poses several big problems for them. It has both content and the ability to rally people to a cause, or "public outrage."

In October 1999 the government declared Falun Gong a "heretical organization" and blocked Internet access to websites that mention Falun Gong. One of the misunderstandings people have about this crackdown was that it appeared the government objected to them as a religion. The government could not care less about the religious aspect of it. What terrified them was Falun Gong's ability to rally people to show up one day in coordinated demonstrations in cities all over the country.

As a matter of doctrinal significance, Falun Gong is intended to be "formless," having little to no material or formal organization. Practitioners of Falun Gong cannot collect money or charge fees, conduct healing, or teach or interpret doctrine for others. There are no administrators or officials within the practice, no system of membership, and no churches or physical places of worship. In the absence of membership or initiation rituals, Falun Gong practitioners can be anyone who chooses to identify herself as such. Students are free to participate in the practice and follow its teachings as much or as little as they like, and practitioners do not instruct others in what to believe or how to behave.[15] This organizational structure is your very worst nightmare if you are a government bureaucrat trying to find the leader.

Besides content, the censors are also sensitive about websites that let people gather information that they can't edit. That's one of the reasons they don't allow Twitter and Facebook and often cut off Google and Yahoo. They can't get to their servers. But there are Chinese equivalents whose servers can be accessed: Baidu is like Google, Weibo is the Chinese Twitter, YouKu is their YouTube, and Renren is Facebook. They are closely monitored and any "offending" material is quickly removed. The clever young people here then devise code words for what they are discussing and the beat goes on. Lots of zapping went on during the drama of the Chongqing Party head Bo Xilai and his wife who knocked off a Brit over a money dispute! There are, however, many, many examples.

One morning I couldn't download *The New York Times*, so I opened my "hole in the great wall," my VPN, and the reason revealed itself. A long and thorough investigative article on the $2.7 billion in holdings of Wen Jiabao (温家宝), the prime minister whose image is of being in harmony with the people. He showed up at every disaster with his hand microphone, assuring everyone the government is on the job. None of these holdings are directly in his own name but over $1 billion held by relatives, including his very elderly mother who was a schoolteacher and his late father, a pig farmer. They must have been very clever investors to amass such a fortune. Other foreign-devil papers reported that Xi Jinping (习近平), the new president, is said to have over $200 million. Not that much compared to Wen Jiabao? At least the poor guy has ten years to build that up.

TV reception is not exempt from the ever-sensitive and thoughtful government. A few years ago on my TV screen came this announcement: "Dear Subscribers, To Mourn the Qing Lai earthquake victims the State Council of the PRC has announced that April 21, 2010, will be National Mourning Day to express deep condolences (we) suspend all overseas (TV) channels that contain entertainment programs. We hereby express our gratitude for your understanding and cooperation." The announcement was hardly needed on the over one hundred Chinese channels because they all had the same mourning programs showing all day and night. I've even experienced TV news programs being cut off in midstory. A CNN anchor says something along the lines of "tonight in Tibet a monk lit ..." Then the program goes to black screen until the offending material is over, resuming with something innocuous like "today in Colorado."

Incidentally the importation of "overseas channels" through satellite dishes is illegal except in some hotels and a few other places. As someone pointed out, graft is also illegal along with prostitution and crazy driving. To get a dish you need to contact some unofficial guy, who knows a guy, who sends three guys to install it. I doubt that there is a building in all of Shanghai without a dish. Several years ago apparently the officials would raid buildings with a cherry-picker crew and just go up and down pulling them off. No more. Friends in the United States often send me stories and news clips as if they don't exist in China. In most minds we are still "far away" and probably not getting news. We get CNN, BBC, CNBC, etc., by satellite dish. I even watched the Super Bowl on local TV without all the ads.

This year someone in Beijing decided there was too much frivolity on TV and cancelled many of the game shows and soap operas. Can you imagine? Nanny where are you? My beloved Singapore handles things a bit differently. They own all the TV channels and hence can more smoothly manage content. Their view, and I suppose the Chinese view as well, is that media is an organ of the state. Free press? What a frivolous idea.

Everything isn't black and white and inflexible. Consider the National

Day movie.¹⁶ Periodically a new movie about the New China will be made, and around National Day (October 1) it will be shown in almost all theaters for several weeks. I find them quite interesting, because it shows what the leadership thinks of itself and its own history.

There have been changes over the years in the perception of history. For example in the 2009 movie *The Founding of the Republic*, Chiang Kai-shek and his son are even-handedly portrayed, not shown as devils. When I mentioned this to a friend he said, "You should have seen it a few years ago." Ha, ha: how times change. China is in a big effort to normalize its interactions with Taiwan, and no doubt the movie purposefully softened the edges of Chiang.

To my surprise it also humanized Mao. Mao in one scene gets drunk and Zhou Enlai sings. Mao grows tired, sleeps, argues with his fellow revolutionaries, and overall is presented as a living person instead of a demigod. His overall strength of character and undiminished drive are also portrayed. This is in sync with the gradual acknowledgment that he wasn't perfect and made some catastrophic errors like the Great Leap Forward and the Cultural Revolution.

The movie highlights the whole subject of how China views and handles the media. For example in the movie cited above, many A-list actors appear such as Jackie Chan and Jet Li, Zhang Ziyi of *Crouching Tiger, Hidden Dragon*, action-movie director John Woo, and many others. They do this for no pay and are glad to be included. But this could never happen in most other countries; the government clears the theaters of almost all the other films showing at the same time and makes them play the National Day film. This caused a bit of an uproar when one of the films kicked off the screens, at least temporarily, was *Avatar*. This arbitrariness leads to local ridicule and undermines the authorities at the very time they are seeking the opposite result.

Am I really affected by any of this in the bright lights and modernity of Shanghai? No. Is there a very soft hum in the background? Absolutely. The state is always there; if not in blatant intimidation, sometimes it taps into what seems to me an undertow of brute force. I've never been threatened or even seen someone being the object of violence. My knowledge, if you can call it that comes from local websites that show "fights" and "attacks," along with scantily clad damsels and gross government fraud. Sometimes I hear locals blaming things on "country people" but it seems even government entities can be prone to physical abuse—punching, kicking, and generally abusing people that have crossed them in some way.

Chen Guangcheng, the blind lawyer who fled to the United States, is a pretty stark, although not isolated, example. The officials just didn't like him saying they were doing anything wrong, so why not teach him a lesson?

I had an experience in the United States when a landlord was inappropriately withholding an apartment deposit from some Chinese students. The only remedy was going to small-claims court. As one of the girls pointed out to me, "in China we would settle this by sending a few strong friends over." I could see the efficacy after they took it to small-claims court and lost when the landlord made up bogus damage and the lackadaisical judge went along with it. It was injustice. The landlord preyed on foreign students from the University of San Francisco with full knowledge that they would return to their home country after graduation and not have the time needed to undertake a real lawsuit. Most foreign students have to leave in six months if they don't have a job and a change in their status. This owner would dream up fantasy damage and claim the deposit. I'm sure this happens all the time, and not just to the youngsters I knew. I too am guilty in that after the first foray into small-claims court I didn't try and follow up, other than calling the USF housing office and getting her removed from their approved list of local apartments. I'm sure it didn't do much good, but maybe I'll make it a project when someday I return to San Francisco.

There are various clips on YouKu, the YouTube of China, of people in restaurants who hit the servers because they don't like the service or someone in a very minor car accident that ends in a wrestling match. What is also quite amazing is that inevitably almost no one comes to help, even when someone is being mercilessly hurt. Is it almost a corollary of Deng Xiaoping's comments after Tiananmen that if some were hurt it wouldn't matter if one million were—we have plenty of people. This appears to be the same attitude by both sides in the civil war before 1949 where hundreds of thousands died in the front lines but the attitude, at least expressed by Chiang Kai-shek to US general Stilwell, was that it was fine since they were just peasants and there were plenty more where they came from.

There is another aspect of this and it is that there is little one can do to redress government action, no matter how outrageous. That is one of the main complaints against the current system—the lack of real countervailing power outside the Party. At least it appears that way to me. If you are an official you can act with impunity against the general public. A little of this seems to have rubbed off on my bank (or maybe just banks everywhere). Maybe this thuggish attitude isn't always meant to be overly imposing. Maybe it is just how unsophisticated people interact. Many a time I've seen a small crowd gathered and people in the center arguing about something quite heatedly. All played out in public. On an airplane flying within China there was a couple with a very small baby and they played a little tune on a music box to keep the child from crying. A man a few rows away burst out and yelled at the father, "Can't you turn that thing off?" Put on your earphones buddy, was my thought, but the father's was even better. "Weren't you ever a baby?" he retorted. The guy shut up.

ॐ ॐ ॐ

However, any time you think China is bad, welcome to North Korea. I recently had, bizarrely and unexpectedly, a chance to visit North Korea, a Communist country that practically makes China look like a democracy. I was quite surprised when in 2010 I was told by the American embassy in Beijing that they had no objections to my traveling to North Korea. (Especially surprising since former President Bill Clinton had weeks before brought home three Americans who had been jailed for trespassing.) Sometime before I had seen an ad to travel to North Korea in a Chinese newspaper. It was a tourist agency run by some Brits and they had been doing the tours for about ten years. After a few queries I said, "Sign me up."

There is no feeling quite like staring across the thirty-eighth parallel knowing you are on the "wrong side" of it because the soldiers staring back are American or South Korean.

The North Korean tour leader for our little group said to me, "Of course I expect the United States to attack us." When I asked why in heaven's name we would want to do that, she said, "You want to invade China." If she were not so smart and so attractive and so friendly I could have thought she was ignorant. She wasn't. She was just badly informed. I realized after spending some quite enjoyable time chatting with her while our bus headed down the empty four-lane highway to Panmunjom that trying to persuade her of other views was fruitless.

She had a master's degree in something like tourism and clearly was very smart. It wasn't surprising that someone who was assigned to take Americans around for four days was committed in thought and deed to what she had been taught. I asked how she could get a master's degree without the Internet and studying foreign literature.

"We have the intranet, just for North Korea."

"But there must be some texts you need to study outside of Korea?"

"In those few instances I could go to a central place and apply for a certain library to be accessed and a certain text, and the authorities would let me go on the Internet and look at it."

We discussed various things, including her firmly held belief that it was the south that had started the Korean War by invading the North, not vice versa, and how their Great Leader Kim Il-sung had beaten the Japanese into surrender in World War II.

"Have you ever heard of the atomic bomb?"

"Yes, but Kim would have made them surrender anyway."

You get the drift; this young woman has a body of knowledge gathered in a closed society. She has no outside references to check if her information is correct or not. Just for the record Kim was thought to be in Russia when World War II ended. Japan had ruled Korea for over forty years. I once discussed understanding North Koreans with former governor Bill Richardson of New Mexico, who had taken several successful trips to North Korea. He told me the problem with dealing both with Kim Il-sung and his son Kim Jong-il was they had no experience or understanding of the outside world. "Plus they are crazy" he added.

I had brought a small iPod to play music, as it was one of the approved items, along with single-shot cameras. Phones had to be left home, along with video cameras. I expect they knew almost all cameras take video as well but that wasn't acknowledged. I asked my guide if she would like to borrow the iPod to listen to some symphonies, which she had said she liked. I pointed out that my iPod also contained the audio book of Obama's *Dreams from my Father*. I asked if she wanted to listen to that as well. She said no. When she returned it three days later I took a look at what had been played and indeed she listened only to the music. No Obama.

I asked my guide once if she was ever able to travel outside the country, and she said that when she achieved a higher rank she could.

"Where?"

"Beijing."

I had to laugh and said, "How about Paris?"

She smiled the smile of a knowing girl.

Before we entered North Korea our group of about fifteen Americans was given an hour lecture on do's and don'ts including what we could and couldn't bring in. We couldn't take photos of any military person or out of the bus windows. Don't fold the newspaper in your hotel room because inevitably every day there will be a photo of Kim Jong-il, and it would be considered an insult to the Dear Leader to be folded over—from which harsh consequences might ensue. Like we might all be kicked out of the hotel. We had to bow at the large imposing statue of Kim Il-sung and place flowers at the base of it. We had to do the same at his "preserved" cadaver on display in their specially designed sarcophagus (looking just as waxen as Mao or Ho Chi Minh, both of whom I had seen). After a few days into the trip it appeared almost all the don'ts were overlooked by our handlers, including taking photos of soldiers.

The trip consisted of staying three nights at the Yanggakdo hotel, which is on a small island in Pyongyang's Taedong River. It is a decent, no frills hotel for foreigners. We were told we could not stray from the grounds although with only a bridge and the river on all sides I'm not sure where we could have gone anyway.

I'll leave you with this image. On the last day of our visit some of our younger fellow visitors urged our guide to stand up and use the bus microphone and sing a song to us. After much urging, hand clapping, and feet stomping, this lovely young woman stood up and started to sing "Arirang," often considered the unofficial national anthem of both Koreas. It is about reunification, told through a song about a wife whose soldier husband has gone off to war and she longs for his safe return. Dead silence in the bus as she sang slowly and beautifully with such heartfelt feelings that tears were not far from us all.

I've had experiences in other parts of Asia that were much more intimidating and scary, at least in the past. I was in Phnom Penh with a group from Singapore, which had gotten together to help build some new houses for a small village. Phnom Penh is a city with a dreadful past—that of the Khmer Rouge who took over Cambodia in 1975 and pushed almost everyone out and into the countryside. It wasn't like any other transformation when one power supplants another such as when the Communist armies marched into Shanghai in 1949. This was on a scale of inhuman suffering and methodical murder. The very day the Khmer Rouge entered Phnom Penh people were ordered out of their houses and if they happened to wear glasses they were shot then and there. Why? Because if you wore glasses you were obviously an intellectual and didn't belong in the new agrarian state. The Khmer Rouge killed university professors and anyone it arbitrarily suspected might not approve of pushing the society back to the Middle Ages.

On the very day I arrived, a disturbing event occurred. There was some government action that would have seemed fairly innocuous anywhere else, but in Phnom Penh the whole city seemed to freeze for a brief few minutes. Afterward, I asked a local what had occurred and they said, "We thought that it might be starting again." That's how traumatic the years under the Khmer Rouge were.

I used to have kidnap-and-ransom insurance when I was active in Southeast Asia. One aspect of it was you could never tell anyone you had the coverage. When I traveled to Manila on business, there was a disconcerting need for a high degree of security, especially if you were a prominent Philippine businessperson. When you visited various corporate headquarters in the Makati business district there were lots of private guards with shotguns. The father of a young family I knew in Singapore headed a prominent insurance company, and I asked why he was in Singapore, not Manila?

"I'm afraid of being kidnapped," he told me.

I asked, "Who would do that?"

"The police," he answered.

There were gangs of policemen who would pull your car over and then kidnap the passengers. It was strictly a dollars-for-ransom scheme. The Philippines was supposed to be one of those countries that was going to emerge from World War II with both linguistic advantages (namely English) and its connection to the United States. It hasn't happened yet.

Until I spent some time with a London client who was in the kidnap-and-ransom business I had thought it was about black-clad ninjas scaling walls and freeing the poor captive. Kidnap was a business and when some poor executive of Standard Oil was captured and held for ransom there was a theoretical menu. Corporate presidents were worth several million, vice presidents were about three quarters of that, lesser executives even less. They kidnapped; you paid. They released.

The only trouble occurred when the kidnappers were amateurs. That was trouble because they didn't know the system and especially didn't know how to release the captive without either hurting them or getting caught. Most of the kidnap action in those years was in Central and South America. I'm afraid the business has no doubt changed with the Middle Eastern turmoil and dedicated religious zealots.

I would like to alert all possible kidnappers that I no longer have the coverage.

My experience in Indonesia in May 1998, when I visited the country just as it was falling apart, was far more jarring than anything I've encountered in China. At that point (and indeed, until President Obama came along) Indonesia was known, if known at all, by Westerners as the land of Bali, that almost mythical idyllic place for honeymoons and liaisons. Maybe they even used the slang "java" for coffee without the knowledge it referred to an Indonesian island.

In our long-ago history classes I'm sure there was at least a few minutes on the "spice islands," where the British and Dutch warred for years over a few islands that they thought grew the only nutmeg in the world. Along with the trade in cinnamon and cloves, this stimulated a grand bargain in 1667. The Dutch felt they had traded up for some of these islands when they gave away Manhattan. This would not be the first Indonesian deal gone bad, and I have a tale to tell.

In early 1996 my investment fund put some money into a private Indonesian insurance company controlled by the Lippo Group with whom we already had an investment. As I recall the exchange rate to the dollar was about 1,200 rupiah. The rate at which you enter and leave a currency is critical, as you will soon see. In early 1997 the insurance company went public. We had an immediate and substantial paper profit. We were geniuses for about two months. Then the roof fell in.

The famous financial meltdown dubbed the Asian Contagion hit in summer of 1997. Like a virus it spread through Southeast Asia. Economies collapsed along with governments. Multiple long-standing leaders were swept out of office, including the indestructible perennial leader of Indonesia, Suharto. The rupiah hit a low of 24,000 IDR to the dollar and people lined up outside Citibank to make deposits in one of the few banks that didn't collapse.[17] It was chaotic and even though we still had our holding in the insurance company, it was literally worthless.

How does it work? If you exchanged a US dollar and got 1,200 rupiah in exchange for that one dollar, and you use that to buy into a company and later reverse the process to take a profit at 24,000 IDR to the dollar you now have to put up twenty times the original amount of Indonesian currency to equal your original purchase. Not so brilliant anymore. The odd thing is that the insurance company within Indonesia can keep running and indeed still does. It is just that it would take our investment forever to get a good return. Even today the rupiah is at about 9,700.

A relatively routine act really brought it home to me. I went to a food court where I regularly had dinner and before the collapse the average meal cost in US terms about twenty dollars. After the collapse the same meal was about two dollars.

As the economy started stalling, the slow-motion collapse of the Indonesian government was unfolding. President Suharto had over his thirty-one-year reign gradually evolved into a grand kleptocracy with his family and favored friends in the forefront. In early 1998 months before he was forced out he declared that the awarding of bids on the new superhighway toll stations would be open and fair. It was. His daughter was open about the fairness of her winning the award. This seemed to be one of the matches that lit the fuse of the revulsion of the general public. Some parts of the country descended into sporadic rebellion and street chaos. Jakarta, the capital, was no exception. One day I was flying across Jakarta in a corporate helicopter and looked down and saw an extensive home with multiple buildings and grounds. I asked a local businessman flying with me if that was Suharto's home. "Yes and we used to not be able to fly over it," he said with a broad smile.

It is quite strange to be a visitor doing business in a country that you know is collapsing. All the outward daily signs are normal. There is a very odd calm. You hear on the radio that a crowd is gathering at such and such a spot and you just avoid it. You see smoke billowing in the distance from a fire and you stay away. You go to appointments and meetings doing your normal routine until it really hits you that your reactions better take a reboot because it is dangerous despite the outward apparent normalcy of the day.

That was brought home for me when the driver who was taking me around the city suddenly floored the accelerator. We sped James Bond style down a street and screeched around a corner and abruptly came to a halt. I was being driven to an appointment in Jakarta.

"What happened" I asked the driver.

"I saw people at the end of the block gathering and it didn't look right," he told me.

Glancing at the floorboards at my feet I realized a small machine gun had slid from under his seat to mine. I realized that I hadn't gotten just a driver. I had a bodyguard. It was time to get out of town.

Nasty things that began as people started to be evacuated—gangs were stopping cars on the way to the main airport and holding them up because they knew people would have lots of cash and valuables as they fled. Fortunately for my local staff I had arranged some seats in a medevac plane that was fueled and ready to go from an undisclosed military airport.

The denouement came when the country opted not to continue the one-man rule and transformed itself into a democracy. Back in the United States in 1999, one late night I tuned my computer to a local Jakarta radio station and listened as the new parliament, vote by vote, elected its first democratically elected President, Abdurrahman Wahid, a blind Muslim leader of the wonderfully named National Awakening Party. He later got rid of the prejudicial laws against Chinese Indonesians. It was really moving after all the turmoil and death to see Indonesia emerge as something completely different from its past and so it remains more than a decade after that thrilling evening.

Sometime later I was at a dinner with economics Nobel laureate Milton Friedman and had him laughing when I told him in Indonesia I had experienced inflation and deflation all at the same time. You learn economics fast investing in multiple countries' currencies. On the brighter side, a little after the crisis my investment bank sold Lippo's bank to AIG as Lippo teetered on the brink of financial collapse. This sale saved them. And the company and family that founded it, the Riadys, endured against odds. During the riots that preceded the fall of Suharto, crowds had marched on and set fire to Lippo's Karawaci shopping center. A few years later flying by helicopter into their headquarters I noticed a new set of buildings next to it and asked the president of the company what they were.

"They are a marine barracks," he said. "No one will ever burn down our shopping center again."

The Riady family still had political power after all the changes. The founding father of Lippo, Mochtar Riady, had once said to me, in the face of impending turmoil. "My family has three strikes against us. We are Chinese, we are Christians, and we are rich."

At the end of the day they still were all three.

---

13. Hukou is a record of household registration by which government permission is needed to formally change one's place of residence. Practically it determines the cost of medical care and other services if you are not a resident where you seek the services. The system effectively controlled internal migration before the 1980s, but subsequent market reforms caused it to collapse as a means of migration control. Shanghai has six million individual nonresidents.
14. All three dissidents' information taken from Wiki list of Chinese dissidents and Chen Guangcheng. Minor omissions and rearrangements.
15. Falun Gong.
16. The PRC was founded on October 1, 1949, with a ceremony at Tiananmen Square. This is when Mao famously announced: "The Chinese people have stood up."
17. Low and high when you are discussing exchange rates can be very confusing. Here low means the value of the rupiah declined in relation to the dollar. So going from 1,200 to 24,000 means you need many more rupiah to own one dollar; hence the buying power has declined or gotten lower. The reverse is true as well. The meal discussed took many more US dollars to buy before the rupiah fell; fewer after.

# Chapter 12

## *Religion*

I came to China believing that religion was suppressed and only a few churches were allowed to operate. But it turns out that I am completely wrong. Freedom of religion in the People's Republic of China[18] is provided for by the constitution with an important caveat. Namely, the government protects what it calls "normal religious activity," defined in practice as activities that take place within government-sanctioned religious organizations and registered places of worship.[19] Most know of the strong Muslim presence in the northwest Xinjiang "Autonomous" Region, and of course Tibetan Buddhists. Many historical Buddhist temples are fully functioning along with Taoist and various other denominations including the old Jewish synagogue. And there are scores of Catholic churches in Shanghai. The Chinese government under its "fundamental laws" prohibits "wizards, witches, and superstitions," it rejects the authority of the Vatican and in a dispute as old as Henry VIII, argues with the church over the appointment of bishops.

According to some evidence, Catholics have been in China since the Tang Dynasty. Christianity has been approved and disapproved using a variety of Chinese descriptive names through various upheavals. Sometimes as a Christian you got right into the Forbidden City and sometimes you had your head chopped off. Sometimes it was accepted and sometimes banned, mimicking the ebb and flow of Chinese history. Today the State Administration for Religious Affairs states that there are 5.3 million Catholics belonging to the official Catholic Patriotic Association, which oversees seventy bishops, and approximately six thousand churches nationwide. In addition, there are roughly forty bishops unordained by the CPA who operate unofficially, and recognize the authority of the Vatican.

One day when I was exploring my neighborhood and walked about four blocks past Jing'An Sculpture Park, I happened upon one of the remaining old Shikumen areas of homes. Shikumen were one of the most dominant forms of housing but are now slowly being replaced by highrise multi-tower developments (like the one where I live). From photos at the gate of my complex it shows that this too was a Shikumen area and no doubt was the park.

Tucked close to the middle of the housing units is the Saint Teresa of the Child Jesus (聖女小德助撒天主堂) Roman Catholic church. Although this ninety-three-year-old building is in complete red-brick harmony with nearby buildings, the church stands out when observed from any of the tall buildings in the area, including mine, because it towers above its surroundings. At street level and wandering through the complicated alley system it is unseen except through a narrow passage because it has buildings that were placed in front of it, effectively blocking it from the street. These buildings no doubt were built during the Cultural Revolution on what looks as if it was a marvelous open plaza. In keeping with tradition the church has an East-West alignment. St. Teresa's is sort of an oasis of the traditional, bordered by the inevitable high-rise towers.

You'd likely expect, as I did, to enter it and find a lovely open space with stained-glass windows, pews, and an altar. Instead, about ten feet into the vestibule you face a cement wall with a barnlike locked door. Where did the area for worship go? It's upstairs. This is really bizarre. How is it that when you enter you don't see the traditional setting? The answer: the Cultural Revolution.

I imagined a story of Sister Hu Li Ling, a nun at the mercy of the revolutionaries. When the band of Cultural Revolutionists burst through the front door, Sister Hu Li Ling raced for the stairs. She made it up six when a teenager grabbed her trailing short black veil and yanked it, pulling her head back and toppling her frail frame backward down the steps. The ruffians in the vestibule kicked her and yelled hackneyed slogans chanted in an almost sing-song way, maybe not even comprehending what they were saying. Sad to say some of the crowd were former students of the nun's. A couple of them pulled her at her legs and dragged her back into the church and propped her on the altar rail.

She was barely conscious. They yelled for her to sit straight and listen to the accusations against her and her religious community, as yet uncaptured. There was the usual litany: foreign agent; dupe of running-dog capitalists; seducer of children's minds; enemy of the New China. She had in fact grown up in the very neighborhood and attended St. Teresa from elementary school through high school. Her uncle had served in the remarkable clinic during the Japanese occupation. But after the revolutionaries started to hit and scream at her, it took only about three minutes for Sister Hu Li Ling to slowly lean to her right and topple on to the marble floor, dead. They moved on, chanting.

This structure, built in 1920, was first trashed, looted, and then converted into a warehouse. Instead of leaving the soaring open atrium the officials added a new floor, cutting off the upward expanse of the church apse. The result is that you enter the worship area only after walking upstairs. A traditional church setting appears but with "stained-glass windows" at just above floor height instead of the lovely windows that once graced the church. These windows have been decorated with colored paper pasted onto the glass. They are probably just the upper sections of full-length windows which were on the floor below. When you look at the windows something strikes you as not quite right and only gradually you realize they are too low.

Life was not easy for religious people, even before the Cultural Revolution or the coming of New China. Close to this spot, where the church was established, two priests were shot for who-knows-what-reason. The impression we get, especially from old movies, and even some more current ones like *The Last Emperor*, is that Shanghai in the roaring '20s and '30s was this souped-up, modern city with one of the world's large financial centers, avant-garde art and music, and money that flowed as easily as champagne in cafe society. We all have seen the posters and photos of lovely ladies in their sexy silk *qi paos* languidly hawking some face powder or cosmetic. All that was real, but at the same time, the country was in the midst of a developing bitter and bloody civil war, the Japanese invasion, the ever-increasing flow of refugees from Russia and Germany, and the rise of gangs like the Green Gang that dominated part of the carved-up city.

A well-known Beijing born artist, Teresa Wo Ye, designed the stained-glass windows for St. Ignatius Cathedral in the Xujiahui section of the city. Three nuns Sisters Wu, Li, and Han worked with her on the fabrication in her workshop at St. Teresa's. Unfortunately she became quite ill and unable to fully complete her work. A controversy surrounding her work arose at the Cathedral in that they depict both Christian and ancient Chinese symbolism. Regardless, they are remarkably beautiful.

When I first discovered St. Teresa's I lost my way inside the building.

This time I was trying to find some good shots for a photo contest being run by the Shanghai Cultural Heritage Administration. I met a nice lady dressed in a simple white pantsuit who kindly took me to various rooms and explained some of the history (which gave me the idea for the sad story of Sister Hu Li Ling). It turned out she is a nun and lives there, along with three or four other nuns and a priest, all stationed in the quarters behind the church building. At present St. Teresa's has a few masses on weekends.

The nuns run a kindergarten and have plans for additional grades. Before the coming of New China in 1949 they had both a grammar school and high school. This was all closed down then and the building went through various incarnations until it was reopened in 1993. Before 1949 they had educated about two thousand students a year, the majority of which weren't Catholics. This valiant group of nuns and priests also established a clinic, which during the war years handled up to eighty thousand people a year. That's more than two hundred a day. A daunting undertaking. They were all arrested and imprisoned in 1949.

It is amazing to think in the midst of all the various upheavals, especially during the Japanese occupation, what the faithful at St. Teresa created and kept going through all the turmoil. From the earliest days until the end of the civil war they kept the primary school for both boys and girls and junior and senior high school going. They even had a group of blind children they tutored in their primary school. The medical clinic served all who were in need.

When I was a kid, I took the name of my hero Francis Xavier as my confirmation name. I have always carried his medal in my suitcase.[20] Francis Xavier died while waiting to sneak into China in 1552, having made it to Shangchuan Island off the coast 125 miles south west of Hong Kong. I've been there and it isn't easy to get to even today (there is marine transportation, in the form of rickety boats, mostly because there is a resort area on the other side of the island).

On Shangchuan there wasn't much to memorialize Francis Xavier, except a very small chapel and some commemorative outdoor walls and sculptures. He died here waiting for Vasco da Gama's son to pick him up and take him into the heart of the imperial kingdom. Poor Xavier was dug up after he was first buried at Shangchuan; dug up and buried multiple times and places. He now "rests" in a glass casket in Goa, although his right arm was carved off and sent to the Jesuit Church of the Gesù in Rome, other bones were sent elsewhere. They should just regather all his parts, bury him once and for all, and really put him to rest.

While I was in the Basilica of Bon Jesus in Goa, India, where St. Xavier is on display, an Indian couple with their child came up and asked my guide, "where is the famous miracle man." I was told that every ten years they take Francis Xavier down and carry his glass casket though the city with huge crowds in attendance. Spare me.

☘ ☘ ☘

It's always nice to meet a real, living saint, which I did in Macau. My friend, the late Father Edward J. Malatesta, SJ, the founder of the University of San Francisco's Ricci Institute for Chinese-Western Cultural History,[21] urged me to go to Macau and meet the Spanish priest Father Luis Ruiz Suarez SJ, who was doing some remarkable work with lepers in China.

Father Ruiz lived most of his ninety-seven years in Macau and founded Caritas Macau to help those in need there. He built a network that later helped sustain scores of leper colonies and homes for children with HIV/AIDS.[22] He survived prison, being banned from China as a possible spy, rode his motorbike everywhere, and was a fan of Real Madrid. Who wouldn't love him? The locals called him "father of the poor" and "angel of Macau." He was that and more.

Many a time I visited him in Macau at Casa Ricci, the Jesuit residence on Largo de Santo Agostinho, a beautiful old Portuguese street. Part of the street was taken up by the residence, and next to it a typical-looking, European-style Jesuit church. Down the block was a complex of buildings housing Caritas.

One night I accepted their hospitality to stay all night in the residence. It was very humble and (unfortunately for me) in perfect keeping of their vow of poverty. The straw mattress kept me tossing and turning all night. The building was built to house more than thirty, and I think at the time I was there it had five. Across the street was a large seminary building that had been closed some time before. Working their many activities, the Jesuits were aging fast and not being replaced in any numbers by young men. What will happen to all the social services and three schools they run when they disappear? Who will take their place?

Father Ruiz was totally focused on his poor. One time after establishing an endowment for the lepers I visited him and expected some praise for what I had done. At least a pat on the back.

Father said, "Russell, I don't like what you have done making an endowment."

Huh?

"But Father it will last one thousand years and generate income every single year."

"No, no they need help now."

I was humbled by his focus and the poor people he served. He was practical. That reminds me of Mother Teresa, who when asked by the mayor of New York, in an expansive gesture what he could do for her, she replied, "Give me a parking place in front of our convent."

Father Ruiz and Father Gregory took me to visit Tai Kam island. This is one of the many venues that the Chinese government used to deposit lepers to remove them from society. Leprosy is still seen in some quarters as a biblical disease requiring permanent quarantine. In fact it isn't even called leprosy in most of the world because of the stigma of the word. It is called Hansen's disease. The truth is, that it is now completely curable before any harm comes to a person, but in China there still just isn't enough knowledge, will, or maybe even medical attention to get it eradicated. The government ceased its policy of sending people to leper colonies in the mid-1980s but either through ostracism in villages or self-exile there remain many active leper colonies.

Tai Kam is about forty miles from Macau off the coast of Guangdong. We took a little outboard motor boat and headed out into the South China Sea, passing fishing boats pulling up full nets and aimed for the open sea. There was nothing there. After what seemed like forever, finally the outlines of an island emerged on the far horizon.

After we landed at the little pier we were greeted by some of the inhabitants. It is hard to describe the horror that goes through your mind when a leper holds his hand out in greeting. Of course you shake hands. Is it like when you think the wing is falling off your airplane but you don't say anything for fear of making a fool of yourself.

Leprosy is a disease that once it progresses can make people quite repulsive, with digits and limbs missing and disfigured faces. A group had gathered in the chapel for mass and they displayed every possible disfigurement. What was surprising to me is that as the day went on their disfigurement faded and they began to be seen as just regular people going about the business of life. They had wives and children, housing provided by the Jesuits and the wonderful nuns from India who lived there. They had vegetable gardens, playgrounds and what you would expect of a very small community. They just were on an island in the middle of nowhere. The Chinese government provided a rice allotment and some other help. During my visit I used a small sketchbook I carried around to do a picture of the area. While doing so, a very young boy named Gam watched me and then asked if I would include him in the drawing. I did.

Father Gregory told me an amusing story. He said that every once in a while the local government official in charge of the area would steal their little boat that was used to transport people and goods to and from the island, the same kind of a boat we were using that day. Father Gregory said that the official would periodically gamble and of course lose. He would then arrange the theft of their boat and sell it to meet some debts. When I asked Father Gregory if he minded, he replied, "That's just doing business in China."

He did, however, tell me about the time the very same official shorted the rice allotment. The three sisters, not one over five feet tall, got in the boat, went to his office and as Father Gregory tells it, whatever they said to him—no one knows—the official is still trembling. He never shorted the rice again!

When we were getting ready to leave in the late afternoon, a small group gathered on the pier to see us off. Father Gregory said that they wanted to say something to me in thanks for the help I had given. They gathered around me. Here was a group tall and short, shirtless, in some cases toothless, some disfigured and they started to sing. A Texas cowboy song about the Red River Valley, sung in Chinese. I have never been so touched. Tears flowed all around.

A friend in the TV documentary field, at my request, agreed to do a program showing the work of Fr. Ruiz and the others in China. I arranged the financing and the idea was to use the program to raise funds. Fr. Ruiz demurred. He said something along the lines of "Russell, it might make the Chinese government mad to expose their problems. Just leave it alone. We will raise funds somehow." He knew well that the government sometimes acted without a lot of information, even bizarrely barring him as a spy for a while. It was so ridiculous a charge that they later removed the ban. At that time of course Macau was still under Portuguese control and you had to get a visa to get into China, even though Macau is literally across the street.

Although I've already mentioned his accomplishments, let me finish up by recounting a few more things this humble man did. According to the people at Caritas he looked after more than eight thousand patients taken care of in 139 centers; helped the families and children of the lepers; arranged for fifteen roads to be built, seventeen schools, five bridges. Because of him seven mobile clinics were manned and operated, twenty-five systems put in place for clean drinking water, and twenty-one systems for electricity.

I last saw him in 2011, his body gnarled by age, confined finally to a wheelchair instead of his beloved motorbike, but his spirit vibrant and inquiring. As our visit finished I asked for his blessing and knelt in front of his wheelchair. He whispered a brief prayer and raised his right arm as Xavier had, and blessed me. He received greetings in heaven a few months later.

**18**. The constitution of China states "Citizens of the People's Republic of China enjoy freedom of religion. No state organ, public organization, or individual may compel citizens to believe in, or not to believe in, any religion; nor may they discriminate against citizens because they do, or do not believe in religion." This protection is extended only to what is called "normal religious activity," generally understood to refer to religions that submit to state control via the State Administration for Religious Affairs. The Constitution further forbids the use of religion to "engage in activities that disrupt social order, impair the health of citizens, or interfere with the educational system of the state. Religious organizations and religious affairs are not subject to any foreign dominance."

**19**. Arriving in China during the Tang dynasty (618–907) the earliest Christian missionaries from the Church of the East referred to their religion as Jǐng jiào (literally, "bright teaching" 景教). Originally, some Catholic missionaries advanced the use of Shàngdì (literally, "The Emperor from Above" 上帝) as being more native, but ultimately the Catholic hierarchy decided that the more Confucian term, Tīanzhǔ (literally, "Lord of Heaven" 天主), was to be used, at least in official worship and texts. Within the Catholic Church, the term *ging jiao* (literally "universal teaching" 公教) is not uncommon, this being also the original meaning of the word "catholic."

**20**. Cofounder of the Society of Jesus. He was a fellow student of Ignatius of Loyola in Paris and one of the first seven Jesuits when they formed their little band of Companions of Jesus at Montmartre in 1534. He led an extensive mission into Asia, mainly in the Portuguese Empire of the time. The Jesuits arrived in Macao in the 1560s. Today's logo image of Macao is their Cathedral of St. Paul begun in 1582 and now only a facade.

**21**. The center was named after the famous Jesuit Matteo Ricci who arrived in Macao in 1582 and then lived in various cities throughout China. In 1601, Ricci was invited to become an adviser to the imperial court of the Wanli Emperor, the first Westerner to be invited into the Forbidden City. This honor was in recognition of Ricci's scientific abilities, chiefly his predictions of solar eclipses, which were significant events in the Chinese world. There is a statue of Ricci in Shanghai in Xujiahui. One of my friends grandfather's grandfather raised chrysanthemums in this very area in the 1800s. It now is one of the most busy and built-up shopping areas in Shanghai.

**22**. Father Ruiz worked with refugees and founded the first housing in Macao specifically established to house the elderly. The Ricci Centre for Social Services evolved into Caritas Macau. Under Caritas, Father Ruiz opened five centers throughout Macao that provided services for the mentally disabled. During the 1980s, he began working with lepers in Guangdong province with the help of an order of Catholic nuns, the Sisters of Charity of St. Anne. He first went to Tai Kam Island in 1986 where 200 lepers had been exiled.

# Chapter 13

## *Let's Eat*

Some friends wonder if it is the food that keeps me in Asia. The answer is complicated. On the one hand, I could tell you about my friends Ivy and Ho Seng's farm, Bollywood Veggies, north of Singapore in the Kranji countryside. I've wandered the fields and ponds of their property, getting the full experience in tasting and learning, especially when Ivy or Ho Seng pick something from a bush or the ground and say, "Try this," and I encounter something sweet or tart or chewy but always new, fresh, and bound to expand my palate. On the other hand, I can tell you about the time more than ten thousand dead pigs came floating into Shanghai's water, followed closely by scores of dead ducks.

And on still a third hand, I can recount the peculiar joys of breakfast in Vietnam. When I was running Spirit of Enterprise Vietnam, my regular server in Hanoi would approach my table in the open lobby of my hotel and ask, "do you want fruit, eggs, or Phở?" Phở consists of a nice size bowl of broth, rice noodles, a few scallions or other herbs, and usually chicken or beef.

If I said, "Eggs," off he went straight out the hotel's open front door, only to return a few minutes later with a steaming bowl of Phở. The next day he would again present his verbal menu and no matter what I answered, I got Phở. No great hardship there; I loved it. I concluded he had no idea what he was asking, but it was merely a polite act and he would hustle for your breakfast, which of course would be Phở because that is what everyone in Vietnam had for breakfast. Phở is readily available from street vendors as well; the only little concern is you can see they "wash" the dishes by hand in cold water, just sort of swiping them around. The chopsticks get the same treatment so I always ordered a glass of hot water, not to drink, but to sterilize my chopsticks. When traveling, I am always armed by my multiple-alphabet hepatitis shots.

For breakfast in Shanghai, I don't often eat out but when I do one of my favorite foods is Jianbing, which is a crepe that has "immigrated" from north China. It is filled with chopped green onions, one or two eggs swirled around and cooked when the crepe is flipped over, and some sweet plum sauce, and a few other sweet and tart ingredients are added. Then the crepe is folded like an ice-cream cone and dropped into a plastic bag; you work from the top down eating this wonderful concoction. There is always a line. The lady with her portable griddle disappears about ten in the morning. She has two competitors nearby, the lady next door who serves triangular crepes with some filling, and the husband-wife team who all day makes round, very greasy biscuity cakes. All the stands get lots of action.

Many Shanghai locals eat out every day. I might do so two or three times a week. You can eat "out" by eating in, ordering lunch or dinner from a very competent local American entrepreneur who has a restaurant delivery service called Sherpa's. Go online or telephone and order from a whole variety of restaurants and it will be delivered to your door, usually within about forty-five minutes. There are a few of these services, and they are especially helpful for parties, when it is raining, or when you just don't feel like cooking dinner.

Shanghai has tens of thousands of restaurants. The higher-end ones all serve wine from the over one thousand wine importers doing business here. As one might expect in a city that has more than twenty-three million people there is every conceivable kind of food on offer. Even cuisines you may not expect to be here—like Mexican or Texas barbecue—name it and no doubt there are multiple restaurants serving that food.

One of my favorite spots is AnaMaya, a vegetarian restaurant in a small house, run by a Japanese woman who cooks, explains the menu, and carefully sources all the fresh food that changes with the seasons. The dining room is decorated with an eclectic blend of Tibetan and Nepalese items, with hanging scrolls and Buddhist images. The music is quiet, just instruments and chanting, consistent with the rest of the decor. There are only about eight tables and a few couches. My former yoga instructor teaches next door and the restaurant draws a community of people interested in Indian mysticism that use the venue to gather when the restaurant is closed. (3 Taojiang Lu, 桃江路3号 Lu, off Hengshan Lu, if you're looking for it). Another is Zen Lifestore, just around the corner on DongPing Lu. It is a coffee house masquerading as a ceramics shop. You have to go through the ceramics shop and then upstairs into a very small and cozy setting with books, wonderful prints, and 1950s music. When was the last time your heard Peggy Lee singing "Fever"? Although there are loads of other wonderful places in many categories, I like the quiet and peaceful solace both venues emit. Not unexpectedly they are in the former French Concession.

For lunch or dinner I often head for the local Chinese restaurants. What I've gradually learned is that there are multiple ethnic dishes along with set regional offerings. There are generally seven main categories of Chinese dishes, but I don't really know all the differences except for Sichuan and what we call Cantonese and Shanghainese.[23] I've learned that the Chinese food in America for the most part is not authentic and is modified for local taste, which is okay but definitely different from what is on offer here.

On the way to dinner I might pass by in my neighborhood the lady who sells cooked duck, always on display in her small, glassed-in, portable cabinet. They are hanging from their heads, skinless and crisp brown. There are many authentic but exotic dishes in restaurants that I have tried once, like fish head, the balls of chicken feet, pigs trotters, bird heads, and so on. One try has been just fine, thanks.

I thoroughly enjoy the variety of dishes, but they are always too much if you are alone. Because not many Chinese eat a meal alone the portions are designed to have multiple people enjoying multiple dishes. Sometimes when a visitor comes I'll take them to one of the many veggie restaurants or a "China lite" one like Din Tai Fung, which specializes in dumplings. If they are adventurous I might take them to Yang's Dumplings, which serves the best Xiaolong Bao in Shanghai. These are dumplings filled with pork and a light soup broth that you first coax out by using your chopsticks to punch a few holes in the dumpling and let it spill into your spoon for a good slurp before you eat the dumpling. Places like Yang are authentic with long lines and crowded tables shared with many other slurping, chomping, loudly talking companions.

It's a little unsettling when the waiters come to the table and stand and wait until you have made your decision on a menu that may not be in English (or if it is will have the writing in quite small letters). I know we have the opposite problem sometimes in restaurants in the United States—when you can't find a waiter to take an order—but this can be disconcerting and doesn't seem all that efficient. A Chinese friend explained it by saying that the waiter is supposed to know the dishes and advise you on your choices. I have watched as friends will take their time as they page through the menu and discuss various dishes with the waiter. Maybe another explanation is that waiters don't get paid very much so a restaurant can have lots of them standing around.

The most unusual story I can tell about a waiter and a local Chinese restaurant is one who, when he saw one of the group of friends at the table with Ayn Rand's *Atlas Shrugged* began a conversation with the reader. It soon developed that the waiter was extremely well read in English and Chinese literature and liked his job because it gave him lots of free time to read. Before the conversation was all over they had discussed Milton Friedman's economics, the US Federal Reserve policy, and various books, and he still had time to take and serve the dinner order. This is clearly unusual as most of the staff tend to be "immigrants" from elsewhere in China. The slang epithet for poor service is that they obviously are "country people, not from here." In Singapore a comparable slur is "they must be from China."

The opposite of this interactive exchange about books and reading is seeing a couple at dinner, not talking at all but all the while tapping on their cell phones. I even saw two guys eating lunch sitting across from each other, both on their phones for most of the meal. I assume they weren't talking to each other. Mobiles during meals is distracting and, I think, rude, but I might as well relax because universally in China, if a phone buzzes, no matter where the owner is, they will answer it and chat along as if they aren't sitting at the table with you. I've seen this not only at meals but in public forums, and even once in church.

I do cook at home, which means I spend some of the time shopping for food. Western supermarkets and organic sellers are my sources of choice, even though I've been told the stamp of "certified" organic on some supermarket vegetables and fruits is not worth anything. Carrefour, the French multinational hypermarket, is the answer in Gubei (a residential area in the Changning district). It has one floor for food and the other for drugstore-type items. A moving ramp between floors rivets your shopping cart to the floor as you slowly descend.

This market is such a jam-packed space that to find anything is serendipitous. I met my match looking for soy milk. First one lady took me to the milk. No soy. Then another found half pints—too small but loaded up on them. Then I found the Angel of Carrefour, a young woman who could find anything. She spoke very little English but she had a thumb of fire on her cell phone, shooting her answers at hyper cyberspeed. She would signal me to follow and she would race down an aisle and I would follow to the destination. "I need"… bam, bam, follow me, down this aisle, over there, back over here, down this escalator. "Do you have?" … bam, bam … follow me, down the aisle, take a left, middle of the row, down one level. She was pretty and very good humored. "It's my job," she kept protesting as I would effusively thank her with each treasure found.

But other than foreign-owned outlets like Carrefour, I've never seen what might be called a supermarket. There are wet markets all over and they provide the shopping needs of local households in their neighborhoods. Wet markets have full range of vegetables, fruits, meat slabs, live fish, turtles, frogs (or croakers as they are called), and various other unidentifiable delights often still alive. On almost every block there are small (usually twenty-four-hour shops) that have some staples and sweets to attract you to buy something you shouldn't, like a candy bar. The other "hook" to get you to come in is they are a place you can pay all your local bills like phone or electricity, as well as top up your cash card. These are the equivalents of what we call "mom and pop stores."

It is not always easy to be understood even when you are in a small shop. These are definitely English-free zones. I was in one of these local stores and tried to find honey. No luck. Tried explaining it. No luck. Finally imitated a bee flying around—success! This was well before I downloaded a life-saving app on my mobile with an English-Chinese translation system.

There are also pop-up food stalls that appear in the morning, transform themselves for lunch and dinner, and then disappear down an alley until the next day. These seem to have regular customers, just like the flatbed truck that comes into our compound twice a week full of fruits and vegetables and unloads for about an hour and then drives off—no doubt for another venue. These itinerant sellers appear and disappear just as the bicycle flower-sellers and various other instant entrepreneurs do.

I've been told that the local street markets have three prices. One for regular customers, one for Chinese who are not regular customers, and one for foreigners. Of course you can bargain in these markets, but even then I would not get the best price. The street sellers all quote outrageously silly prices to foreigners, but as soon as you show you know the score they get somewhat more reasonable. It is all somewhat of a futile tussle over what is in the end, very little. What is a ¥3 or ¥4 discount—only about fifty or sixty cents? But it is the principle of the thing, or so I tell myself as I negotiate with my local man who would never let me have an avocado for ¥8. The marked price ¥12 and the selling price will be ¥9.

There are also English-language grocers online who will deliver and you can pay with Paypal. The one I use is called Fields and focuses on organic produce and working with local providers who meet quality standards. It probably costs about 30 percent more than local grocers but getting real organic food in China is a test of will and integrity. There is, as in the United State, a certificate given to properly vetted organic farms but there are multiple seals and none are foolproof so I rely on Fields to sort it out. Not only do foreigners worry about the quality of the food but so do Chinese.

And they should. How would you like your pork, duck, or chickens? Stir fried or thoroughly soaked in the river? Not long ago the threat of H7N9 came to the city and the authorities closed all the live poultry markets and killed all the chickens because of this new strain of bird flu. Since pork and chicken are staples of the everyday diet there is some cynicism about what happened to those corpses. Were the pigs and chickens really destroyed or were they sold out the backdoor?

Add to your concerns the melamine-poisoning scandal[24] from a few years back, the most horrific example of total disregard for the consumer that I can ever remember. Baby formula was being laced with melamine, a chemical that can cause kidney stones and in some cases, lead to the deaths of the babies. More than twenty companies were engaged in this practice. Unfortunately—but not entirely unexpected in China—the original whistle-blower who blew the lid off this scandal was later murdered.

Periodically the civic authorities crack down on the use of reconstituted oil used by many restaurants and street sellers as the basic cooking oil. Reconstituted is just a subterfuge word for oil that has been used by restaurants and discarded, then resold and supposedly cleaned before selling it again. It is illegal—along with fake Louis Vuitton bags and the latest movie CDs.

For water there are multiple dealers who deliver large bottled-water containers that fit on the top of a dispenser. I don't think anyone drinks the water out of the tap. For a few years the water smelled of a chlorine additive but now a new plant has been initiated for the Jing'An part of town and that chemical smell has disappeared. The government of Shanghai has assured us that it is much improved. Various sections of town have discreet water sources but all ultimately comes from the Zhangxi River to the HuangPu River and to us—along with who knows what else? I suppose it might be safe to eat the fish, most of it alive and ready to cook. Then again are these farm-raised fish? No one says. The ultimate answer is order what seems to be carefully sourced and at home cook the daylights out of it.

**23**. The diversity of geography, climate, costumes, and products has led to the evolution of what are called the "Four Flavors" and "Eight Cuisines," but as catering is a living art, subclassifications continue to increase. They are Shandong, Guangdong, Sichuan, Hunan, Jiangsu, Zhejiang, Fujian, and Anhui cuisine. Travelguidechina.com
**24**. China reported an estimated three hundred thousand victims, with six infants dying from kidney stones and other kidney damage, and an estimated fifty-four thousand babies being hospitalized. A number of criminal prosecutions occurred, with two people being executed, another given a suspended death penalty, three others receiving life imprisonment, two receiving fifteen-year jail terms, and seven local government officials, as well as the Director of the Administration of Quality Supervision Inspection and Quarantine (AQSIQ) being fired or forced to resign. Jiang Weisuo, forty-four, the man who first alerted authorities to what would become the melamine-tainted milk scandal was murdered in Xi'an city.

## Chapter 14

*Expo*

The drumbeat for Expo began several years prior to its official opening in 2010. Long ago these exhibitions were known as world fairs. China made this one into a spectacular presentation of its ability to present itself and its products and made all the countries who participated glad they had. I began to be aware of the coming event in 2008 when I saw that the city in many parts was cleaning, scrubbing, painting, paving, and generally putting a fresh face on. Into 2010, construction was halted so there would be no dust, pollution, or noise, and where there were scaffoldings for construction along a main tourist street such as Nanjing Xi Lu, it was covered with a trompe l'oeil rendition of what was to come. Flowering plants were installed on newly painted abandoned walls.

The overall theme of the Expo was "Better City—Better Life." This was plastered all over town in every conceivable method. The mascot was Haibao, a Gumby-looking figure ubiquitous thought the town. Expo ran from May to October 2010 and had the largest participation of any fair in history. A total of seventy-three million people came. That's about 406,000 a day and on one day there were over a million people. The overall numbers belie the fact that close to sixty-nine million were from China. They were bused, trained, flown in from all over the country. The logistics of organization were really exceptionally well done. Can you imagine any city, no less Shanghai which already had a population of twenty-three million, absorbing this kind of flow of visitors over six months and not have huge bottlenecks and howling complaints?

The Chinese utilized a month-long trial period before Expo opened to get it right. People were ticketed in, just to see what was still needed. Lots of ideas emerged, such as adding hundreds and hundreds of guides, more entrance gates, and better coordination with the city's metro and buses. It ended up that there were 1.7 million specially trained volunteer guides. Shanghai even put on the street four thousand brand new cabs painted in distinctive yellow and green; only they could take you right to the front gate. There even were several new metro lines added in the four years prior to the opening, including one that operated just for Expo. Overall the planning and execution was relatively flawless by the time they opened for business.

All this of course meant that from 2002 when they were awarded the 2010 Expo, Shanghai had to clear land in the heart of the city on each side of the Huangpu River to make way for this enormous project. Something like 18,000 families and 270 factories were relocated. When talking to a friend who had lived in the Expo area about their enforced move I asked if they were okay with it. They said they didn't want to move. They liked their old neighborhood even though it was old and run down, however they acknowledged they were given very up-to-date new housing and it was much better than what they had.

Let me tell you, China had it organized. I went three times and each time was able to see multiple pavilions, although when I was on my own it was always the "minor" ones. Saudi Arabia had a 3D surround-screen exhibit that people waited six or eight hours to see. China, Japan, some of the European countries were extremely popular. United States was highly attended, but I didn't go as it was a series of big-screen films of various aspects of the country. Those who did said it was quite all right. The problem in those exhibits with movies is you would be trapped in the film screening while you watched it and then were moved as a group to the next film and the next while some other pavilions like China, Italy, or Singapore let you move at your own pace. The only reason I was able to go to the China pavilion was as a VIP guest of one of the Chinese sponsors. I was joined with some cabinet members from Mongolia. We had VIP guides, no waiting anywhere we went, and of course we visited the Mongolian pavilion with its dinosaur eggs and handmade toys. There was even a Mongolian musical group playing their national songs. All in all there were more than two hundred pavilions, sponsored both by countries and corporations and on any one day you could probably only have time and energy for four or five.

The China pavilion was especially interesting with its lively long digital scroll depicting an ancient town with the people moving along in their day-to-day duties. This mimicked a famous ancient scroll that was familiar to the Chinese visitors. There was also a short film and some actors doing a modern depiction within a digital building showing today's most advanced architecture. The China pavilion guides were tall young women in designer outfits all perfectly coifed, made up, beautiful, and friendly. Even Singapore Airlines flight attendants would have had a tough time competing with this bunch.

It constantly amazes me that when the government, whether it is the city or the country, decides to do something they can marshal all their forces and capital and get it done. I often remark that the new half span of the Bay Bridge in San Francisco (with Chinese steel) took more than a decade to finish. In 1935 the Golden Gate Bridge and the full original Bay Bridge were built in about two years. What's happening? Well all the environmental sensitivity and studies for one. They take years. I saw one for an Oakland building that cost close to $1 million to prepare and the building itself was less than $10 million. It isn't just environmental reports that slow things down, but there are multiple lobbies who will fight anything with the cynical view that they will get paid off either by the courts for bringing the topic into the public forum or by the party trying to build whatever they want to build. Maybe a little more Chinese-style dictatorial viewpoint is needed. About a year ago Shanghai approved a new Disney amusement park. Six months later a tiny one-paragraph article appeared in the *Shanghai Daily* noting that the one thousand families who had been on the land set for the park had now "been successfully relocated." Can you imagine this happening in less than ten years of fights in the United States?

This, and all the development, has led to a tremendous growth in real-estate values, which are the primary storehouse of wealth for many Chinese. A friend of mine is creating new wealth by purchasing real estate and holding it after doing some renovations and then selling it. She said that she makes the family money for her husband and daughter and is the most successful of her family, which is mostly made up of rural farmers. She and her husband came to the city about ten years ago and after borrowing a few thousand dollars she was able to buy a very small apartment. Gradually she has used the leverage of debt and bought and held about three places so that today she is renovating one that the renovations alone are probably close to $300,000. The real-estate value growth in the Shanghai area has been extraordinary with double-digit growth almost every year for over twenty years. No wonder people think that this is a sure way to build wealth.

When the government wants to stimulate the economy it pours funds into the government-linked banks, which in turn lend it to the developers. Recently one of the results has been many apartments sitting empty just waiting for value enhancement. At the same time some people can't find a place to live in the city. Another reason you can hold and not worry about the apartment being occupied is that until this last year the government didn't impose any carrying taxes, which are common in the West. The land is all owned by the government and buildings have seventy-five-year leases that can be renewed. To dampen speculation and encourage people to lease their apartments they have added some transfer taxes and limits on the number of places you can own. This applies to only three or four cities. It remains to be seen if it will dampen demand. Some families I know are just putting their additional holdings in their children's names. Tighter restrictions apply to foreigners.

Some of my friends have wanted to invest in real estate in the United States, seeing the recent collapse of the real-estate market as an unusual opportunity for investment, but getting a loan to do this is apparently very difficult. Not many people I know invest in any other vehicle than real estate or maybe a little gold. What is amazing about all the growth in wealth from real estate is that it has brought capital to people who before had no way of increasing their net worth.

Speaking of making money, my friend Bob Theleen tells the improbable story of something he saw with his own eyes. It seems ducks are plentiful and are widely consumed on a regular basis by almost everyone. There are huge duck farms but according to some, it is the lean ducks that bring the best market price. Most ducks are pretty fatty so if you can produce lean ducks you have a financial advantage. You could try and breed lean ducks but not the farmer that Bob visited. The farmer's answer: duck treadmills. He had set up multiple treadmills running at speeds just enough not to have ducks fly off them but would have to run like hell to stay on it. These ducks thereby ran off their extra fat and were prized in the market. I know this is hard to believe but Bob swears he saw it with his own eyes. Now let's see. What happens if the power unexpectedly goes off? What if one of the lead ducks just has had it and quits running? The whole thing is hysterically bizarre. Let's hope for the poor duck's sake that the farmer gets into genetic engineering.

# Chapter 15

## *The Woman's Dilemma*

"What about the women," my male friends often ask. "That's what keeps you there, right?"

I hope they don't assume I am like one of my friends who relocated to Hanoi. He frequented massage places and karaoke clubs where "dates" come with the price of the room. He is a business genius and created a thriving company in Vietnam and had "wives" there and in Thailand. I met his Vietnamese "wife" and never quite knew what she did for a living. We once went to her home, which was on the street floor; and indeed you sat on cement and ate dinner that was cooked with an open fire and wok. As you sat circled around the wok the food would be dispensed. His "wife" in Bangkok was really lovely, but as I gradually realized, a hooker. He had met her in some dance bar where girls dance with numbers attached to their bras—you choose; they drink and go home with you. She later moved to Switzerland. He was fine with that.

One early evening when I was walking in Shanghai to a restaurant, a lady pedaling a bike up MaoMing Lu drew parallel to me and offered sex for sale. It was so unexpected I just burst out laughing at the preposterousness of it all. Did she want to do it on the bike? She laughed too and then pedaled off up the dark street. Then there was that time I was in Macau for an international insurance conference, staying at a convention hotel where there were ladies of the night stationed at the counter of the hotel's coffee shop, in the lobby, at the entrance, and even around the shops. They were the canapés lazing around for the gamblers and hotel guests to pick up. When I rode the elevator up to my room, on an intermediate floor a lady got on who obviously had just finished a job. She immediately offered to accompany me to my room. Now that's express service. I demurred!

But the beautiful women certainly add to the tapestry of life in China and beyond. I'm inclined to say that people are the same the world over, but I don't actually believe that. There are vast differences, in my observation. America has Marilyn Monroe, but Chinese culture celebrates its beautiful women in myth and fable like nowhere else. Justly in my opinion. Like Italian opera, China has many wildly romantic stories of most beautiful ladies who die, fly to heaven, are buried and unburied, and are separated from their love by the Milky Way, only to be reunited once a year as birds make a bridge for them.

Consider the famous Four Great Beauties, which Wikipedia describes as four ancient Chinese women renowned for their beauty. With scarce historical records, their stories have been embellished over the centuries, but they influenced kings, emperors, and ultimately Chinese history. Three of the Four Beauties brought kingdoms to their knees, and the lives of all four ended in tragedy or under mysterious circumstances.

The Four Great Beauties lived in four different dynasties, each hundreds of years apart. In chronological order, they are:

> **Xi Shi (西施沉魚)**, c. seventh to sixth century BC, Spring and Autumn period: said to be so entrancingly beautiful that fish would forget how to swim and sink away from the surface when she walked by.
> **Wang Zhaojun (昭君落雁)** c. first century BC, Western Han dynasty: said to be so beautiful that her appearance would entice birds in flight to fall from the sky.
> **Diaochan (貂嬋閉月)** c. third century, Late Eastern Han/Three Kingdoms period: said to be so luminously lovely that the moon itself would shy away in embarrassment when compared to her face.
> **Yang Guifei (貴妃羞花)** 719 to 756, Tang dynasty: said to have a face that puts all flowers to shame.

There are multiple stories of beauties bringing down emperors and or getting bumped off because they are too much of a distraction to the more boring business of governing the country. I'd say one of the beauties of the recent past has been Gong Li (巩俐), who appeared in Zhang Yimou's (张艺谋) first film, *Red Sorghum,* and practically made all the clocks in China stop, as if one of the Four Beauties had returned. Later the "emperor" got into the act with the censors by banning Gong Li's film *Ju Duo* for being "a bad influence on the physical and spiritual health of young people." Yeah, let's go see it!

I think of the Four Beauties sometimes when considering the plight of the modern Chinese beauty. I know a handful of very, very stunningly attractive women between twenty-eight and thirty-eight who share many similar circumstances, the most obvious one being that they are not married. For the most part they have graduated from top-rank universities, have very responsible jobs, speak multiple languages, have a wide range of interests, and frustratingly, cannot find the right person to marry.

I've met some of their boyfriends who, for the most part, seem to me very ordinary compared to the women. They are sort of useful to them since no one else is around. Once, when introduced to one of the boyfriends, I heard him say, sotto voce, to the girl "but you told me he was forty." Ha! How the women torture these guys. It's nice for me to pal around with them and go to the symphony or movies or try a new restaurant (always going dutch at their initiative) and have lots of fun, but I'm not the answer for them; I'm their friend, confidante, and advisor, or even as one calls me, "grandpa" (which is marginally okay).

In one of his meetings with Richard Nixon, Mao decided he had the secret weapon to cause problems to the United States. In talking about Chinese women he said, "Let them go to your place. They will create disasters. That way you can lessen our burdens." He went on: "Do you want our Chinese women? We can give you ten million.... By doing so we can let them flood your country with disaster and therefore impair your interests. In our country we have too many women, and they have a way of doing things."[25]

Is there something about the Chinese man who is intimidated by these ladies? I'm told the men want to dominate their spouse and even though the infamous mother-in-law problem has subsided and the newly married often live in their own apartment, among some there is still pressure to let parents come and live depending on their circumstances.

There are plenty of Chinese girls and women that do get married in the regular course of life, having met their future husbands just as couples around the world do, through friends, former schoolmates, at work, and through family intermediaries.

But in China there are a few interesting twists, including the "mass" dating event where hundreds of eligible girls and boys meet in some kind of speed-dating format. I talked to one of the organizers of such an event and she said that they always have problems finding enough boys to attend. I don't know if it is shyness, lack of good qualifications—job, condo, car—there is a slight imbalance between the number of boys to girls born each year, which should mean more boys showing up, but that doesn't happen.

The courtship and marriage rituals of China vary depending upon the region. Here in Shanghai the young unmarrieds and plenty of MBAs (by that I mean, Married But Available rather than Ivy League business graduates) head for local clubs and bars. The flashiest joints are in and around the Bund. They are packed, have loud, good music and pour large drinks, the three criteria that the girls use to measure the quality of any place.

A young friend is my scholar and reporter on the ways she and her friends meet eligible young men. A girl may be sitting home on a Thursday evening and get a message on her mobile about 9 p.m. that the party of the evening is at M on the Bund, Mint, Muse, or Hollywood: "Gan or Qian has a table. Want to come?" At that point the young woman will spend the next hour getting her makeup on and dress chosen before heading out for an evening of drinking, flirting, dancing, playing games, and hanging out.

In any one night, beginning around 10 p.m. and lasting until the bars may or may not close at 3 a.m., the ladies may hang out in multiple places, moving around as one hot place cools off. They prefer not to go and just stand around in the pool of milling people on high radar alert for the eligible. The best way is to have a friend who has a table usually that seats ten. The "owner" of the table, almost always one or two men, will pick up all the charges and will invite a couple of guys and fill the rest of the spots at the table with lovely young women. Since almost always the blaring of the music prohibits anyone hearing each other, they drink and play table games.

The drinks at the good places are strong and cost ¥80 ($13) for a normal cocktail and several hundred for Chivas or other spirits. The table itself costs about ¥3,000 to ¥4,000 ($500 to $600+) a night and includes two bottles of Chivas or the like and some soft drinks. In a bar a girl I was with once asked if she could have "sex on the beach." Truly, I was mystified, no doubt trying to figure out where the closest beach was.

As I fumbled she said, "That's a drink."

"Oh," I said, trying not to reveal my disappointment.

From time to time two girls may go into the dance pool, which is where the rubric of proper behavior takes place. Since the dance floor is so crowded the girls are all surrounded by other people. If a boy is interested in a girl he will hover, dancing close by in hopes of catching the eye of the girl he is interested in. The girls can easily spot interest and depending on their own inclination and attraction, will or won't at some point turn and start dancing with the boy. When they stop the boy may ask the girl if he can buy her a drink. If she accepts he takes her back to her table and goes and gets it to return and give it to her. Maybe they will swap phone numbers, but he will never seek to sit down since this is not "his" table. If he has his own table it is okay to take her back there for one drink but still, she must return to her primary host table. All this sounds somewhat ritualized but is designed not to have young men challenge each other over a nice girl.

The ratios of men to women almost always favor the men. I've heard the story of a guy who goes to a bar called 秀XIU in an office building named Yin Tai Center in Beijing three nights a week. He has ten to forty girls at his table a night; he sleeps with maybe three a week. He is twenty-seven and in a family business. You get in this bar by knowing someone at a table or you wait one or two hours in a line outside on a Friday or Saturday night. The girls go for fun and they can introduce him to, say, a princeling (the gold standard of connections) if one comes over to their table and says hello. A princeling is most likely a son of a very high government official or grandson of one of the original revolutionaries who with Mao created today's China.

Given scenarios like this, I have asked my women friends, "Can you really meet someone who you want to see another time?" Apparently you can. Generally guys get nothing more than phone numbers in the first encounter. But maybe if a really cute guy turns up at the last place and he's already met the girl either earlier in the evening or on another occasion, then anything is possible—when 3 a.m. rolls around a girl may go home alone, she may go home with him, or she may just bunk down with her lady friends.

But more often than not, the girls say the men they meet at the hot bars are MBAs, young wealthy married guys who are always on the lookout for their next girlfriend. Only after sex do they reveal that they are married. This breaks the heart of some and outrages others, but some girls just carry on reaping the tangible benefits such as bags, trips, and the high life while the guy's wife and/or kids remain unaware of his activities, and often, live in another city.

There is an infamous quote made by a mainland Chinese wife living in Singapore. Her husband, who was in his early thirties and very, very rich, shot through a red light at about eighty miles per hour in his red Ferrari (worth about $1.4 million) and killed himself and two people in a cab he hit broadside. He had a young woman passenger, who lived. His pregnant wife rushed grieving to the scene and asked, "Who is *she*?" a sad inquiry made by many a Chinese wife.

Today many Chinese women don't take on their husband's name nor do they feel they have to accept accommodating him with having the extended family all live together. If they have the money they may buy a new home for the parents to live. In general today's women are expected to realize that in time the husband will run around a bit and even have a girlfriend. There is an insidious phrase, "one eye opened, one eye closed" which means that a good wife is expected to ignore flings and take them just as something that happens in life and not worth disrupting the family over.

I attended many extended dinners in Jakarta with the patriarch of a family and his son during weeks of negotiation over buying an interest in their company. Since I don't drink and such evenings tend to be long and drawn out, I had assigned one of my senior guys to be the official drinker. Over weeks the dinners evolved into the three men drinking and carrying on while the son's wife and I spent long evenings talking. It was quite easy since she was educated, smart, and very sexy. Over time we started talking about her husband's possible affairs.

I must say that I mused "with a wife like this who needs an affair?"
But she was quite clear she thought he was having multiple affairs.
I said, "Doesn't that bother you?"
"No, not at all. Men are monkeys."
What? She felt that this was just the way men were, and so what? Quite intently she added, "However, if any of these affairs ever interfere with the family I will kill him." Gulp. She meant it. So in short if he wanted to have some dalliances that was okay, but if their lovely little family with a wife and two kids was disrupted by some woman, he should be aware she wasn't kidding.

Some of the "beauties" I know won't accept the one-eye-opened, one-eye-closed lifestyle. Others feel unfazed by it. At a dinner with about six young women, one of the ladies pointed out that passion only lasts a few months. One of the other ladies who is thirty-seven and looks twenty-four said, "Well passionate sex only lasts a few hours and then reality settles in." This younger woman I had first met in a university setting when I had given a talk and she came up after to ask my advice. She is charming and quite beautiful and clearly was a standout in the class. Almost a year later I ran into her quite by chance on my way into a Starbucks. We actually reached the door at the very same time and she exclaimed "My mentor!" We visited over coffee and exchanged cards. I invited her to a dinner with the group of "beauties" who I thought she would profit by in meeting since they all had good jobs and were secure in their careers and she was just starting out. Well, boy, was I wrong. It turned out at dinner with the six of us that she was the same age as the others and had an eighteen-year-old son and a daughter. She wasn't a student at all; she just looked like one and had attended the lecture to learn. Since that is where I first met her I had assumed she was a student.

She is divorced and it raises the topic of single mothers and how they fare here. I know two others who are single, both young widows with sad tales. Vivian Li's husband died from blood cancer and the other's husband also died from cancer in his early thirties. Xiaoming is a professional, has a very responsible job—indeed she is a medical doctor doing research—but despite being exceedingly attractive, cannot find the right man. I think partially because she has a son in his early teens. Apparently many Chinese men don't want to raise "someone else's child."

There is another problem with the ladies past their late twenties. There is an insidious term used for them, "leftover women," rather like in Japan where a girl over twenty-five is pejoratively called a "Christmas cake" meaning that the cakes given at Christmas are stale the day after. In theory "leftover women" includes any woman over thirty that was looked over and rejected for some reason and hence without a husband at an age at which you are expected to have a husband. This is not strictly a male viewpoint; I have heard girls talk about their prospects as "leftovers" and that they don't hope for much since probably all the good men are already taken.

My friend Xiaoxiao Zhang's take on this is that eligible men her age (twenty-eight) aren't interested in girls her age because they are still playboys or they want a twenty-two-year-old wife who won't give them trouble by being at all independent. I met Xiaoxiao in 2008 when she volunteered along with another student to help out Spirit of Enterprise in San Francisco while they were getting their master's degrees at University of San Francisco. Xiaoxiao was from Chongqing, China, and Jan Pijjayachan from Bangkok, Thailand. As I got to know the girls I realized how helpful and interesting they were. Jan had a boyfriend, so wasn't as available to explore the culture of San Francisco as Xiaoxiao was. As time went on I showed her the various interesting things that go on in San Francisco (the Gay Pride Parade was an amazement beyond her wildest imagination). Soon Ann Miller helped introduce her to some local professional women and Xiaoxiao was quite comfortable with her situation.

Often I brought her to friend's homes so she could see how people in America lived. At one point she lost her apartment and stayed in my guest room for a little over a month. One result was she made some wonderful dinners and one night prepared a full Chinese dinner with dumplings made from scratch for my guests. Later she moved and got a room of her own in a shared apartment, which seemed to work out pretty well. When she graduated after about a year and a half her parents and cousin came to the ceremony. I think that is when she started calling Ann and me her American parents. It stuck.

Xiaoxiao moved back to China about the time I decided to stay permanently in Shanghai; she in Beijing working for a real-estate firm in the corporate offices and I establishing Spirit of Enterprise China. From time to time we stayed in each other's cities and explored newfound cultural sites together. Several times we took cruises on the wonderful six-star cruise line Ann Miller is general counsel to, Crystal Cruises. Xiaoxiao and I would get cabins on opposite sides of the ship so that if there ever was a sight to see one of us would have a view.

The other reason was to make clear we were as good as "father and daughter" although let me tell you, that doesn't work. No matter what we say, people think we are lovers. This extends to very good friends whom I have explicitly told we are not, and being male, they don't believe a word of it. It gets a bit awkward for poor Xiaoxiao sometimes, but she's a good sport and we know what our relationship is. We both have just decided to ignore the rest of the world and be good friends no matter what anyone thinks.

In terms of getting married Xiaoxiao would love to find a good man and settle down to "a quiet life." Her mom is unrelenting in calling almost every day asking if she has met someone, can she please meet so-and-so, has her aunt called to tell her of this nice boy—it goes on *ad nauseam*. To placate her mother, Xiaoxiao has met with a few of the "good boys" and nothing has come of it. Her current thinking is to head back to San Francisco and settle in there.

I was touched by a story one friend told me. She is about thirty-one and very attractive and doesn't have a boyfriend. She has a responsible job in an accounting firm. She told me she sits home weekends and sometimes breaks into tears because she doesn't have anyone. I just can't figure it out. Some of these women work in companies large enough that there must be some eligible men. In Japan they practically force the university graduates together. They encourage dating and marriage among employees and of course expect the girl to disappear at the first pregnancy. Here there is the mother in the background literally hounding the daughters to get married and get them a grandchild. It puts the girls in a state of mind to literally grab any even vaguely worthwhile guy. One friend startled me by saying, "All I need a man for is to make a child. I want him to be healthy, have a good job, and fulfill his role in the family. That's enough. Maybe love will follow." What a different outlook to the American view of love first and a relationship may follow.

Others I know don't have that outlook and have clashed with their mothers and even don't talk to them anymore. They plan their career and concentrate on it, having affairs now and then, even with married men, but remain focused on their own lives. With the one-child policy this is a very hard stance for the woman. There are so many intertwined social and family "musts" surrounding having a child.

But let's assume a young Chinese woman has found the right guy. Who is he? He has to be about the same economic and social status. A princeling is unlikely to marry down if his father has high office. He will marry either a very rich girl or the daughter of another princeling or high official.

In America the tradition has been that the girl's family pays for the wedding but in China it is more complex. Actually the guests put up most of the wedding costs with red envelopes given at the wedding meal. You figure out how much your red envelope should contain from how large the wedding is expected to be and the kind of hotel they've chosen for it.

In Shanghai there is a popular song—supposedly a spoof but actually on the mark—saying don't come near me unless you have a good job, a car, and a condo. Many young women today won't marry a guy who doesn't have his own place. They have no interest in living with his parents. It is even growing more common that they already are living together in their own place prior to the wedding. So who gives the BMW and who gives the condo? The wife's family will probably give a car to the new couple and the groom's family will donate the condo.

Before the wedding meal there is a fun and complex charade played out at the bride's home. The groom and his best men come to the building and amid firecrackers going off, call out to the bride to come out. The bride's family calls back that they won't let her go. More entreaties from the groom follow. Maybe he calls up from outside her high-rise with many kibitzing aunties gathered around watching. This goes on for a while and then he is let into the building. But then he's stopped again at her front door, where he has to plead and beg that her relatives release her. All in good spirits. When he finally gets her out and to the car the whole entourage of relatives and friends join in the fun. The cars are festooned with flowers and paper decorations of the character of double happiness (囍) and it is all quite festive. Before they leave there is a huge blast of fireworks and then off they go.

Either a few days or weeks prior to the wedding they have signed at the registry and are officially married at that point. The ritual photos that the grooms seem to hate and the brides love might have been taken months before, usually in public places like parks or in front of early twentieth-century homes. On a good sunny day in spring you'll see these couples all over town.

I've been to a few wedding banquets and they are pretty much what you would expect. A family friend or senior business or government friend officiating, bride and groom pledging their troth, lots of food and drink, "kiss, kiss, kiss" chanted as the bride and groom greet each table. At one wedding I was surprised at the casual dress of some of the guests, even in T-shirts. No one seemed to mind as others were in suits or more casual sports coats. The meal itself is served in many courses and goes on for hours.

My sympathies go out to my young women friends who are still looking for their groom. The pressure to get married and produce a child is intense, and once a girl leaves university her mother is often unrelenting in expressing the desire that daughter will bring a boy home. I've mentioned this before but cannot overemphasize the constant, unrelenting pressure on young women from their mothers to get married as soon as possible and have a child.

This makes it doubly hard for those self-reliant women that want either a career or independent life prior to or instead of marriage. Many articles are being written about unmarried couples who live in separate apartments but see themselves as committed to each other. Some of my women friends have expressed to me that they are perfectly happy keeping control of their own life and making their own living. Of course this begs the question of whether they will ever have that child their mothers want them to have.

**25**. In a long conversation that stretched way past midnight at Mao's residence on February 17, 1973. US State Department on US-China ties between 1973 and 1976.

# Chapter 16

## *Family Life and Death*

Over time I've heard many family stories that show different aspects of Chinese society. I can't say they are representative but they must not be unique. What often emerges is the strong tie between generations and their deeply felt obligation to their elders, no matter what the circumstances or feelings between them.

A woman I know was severely and methodically beaten by her mother as a child. Her mother had "a bad temper," she said, and would beat her for no reason. When she left home after university she didn't talk to her mother for two years. Today she is independent and makes her living by trading stocks online. She is about thirty and unmarried and controls her own life. Every few months when she has accumulated enough spare cash she takes a long trip, often to Europe. Why no boyfriend, I've asked, and the response seems to be that it is hard for a local boy to handle an independent, stand-on-your-own, woman. When asked what she will do when her mother can't care for herself any longer she said, "I will do my duty."

Another woman, in her late twenties, tells the story of her father's Communist Party membership and his enthusiasm for Mao and why the future was good with the Party in charge. Like any child, she heard stories around the dinner table as she was growing up, and until she was about fifteen took everything he said on faith. Gradually she began to discover that much of what he had promised the Party said it stood for was not true, certainly not for her generation. She had ferocious fights with her father over the years and he was unyielding and so was she. When those who grew up during Mao's time and went through all the turmoil and insanity meet the current generation where Mao is almost a comical characterization in a Warhol triptych, there is bound to be a clash. Today they just don't talk about it anymore, leaving each with their views.

Yet another tells of locking her door at home as she grew into a young woman in her teenage years for concern her father might come in the night. A father who now calls her a "whore" apparently because she hasn't married and is in her late twenties. This is simultaneous with a mother who hectors her almost daily about getting a boyfriend and starting a family.

In families we often hear, no matter what country, struggles over inheritance. In China I have heard of a widowed husband struggling to cut his child out of the mother's will. It sounds so strange when you would expect the parents to adore the one child, but at times when money looms there is trouble.

A story of families sticking together comes from a young professional woman taken in by the ubiquitous Nigerian scam. Frankly I didn't think anyone would fall for this scam but apparently people regularly do. It goes like this. You get an email, usually from Nigeria, that purports to be someone who has been given your name as someone reliable to help them out. They tell the story of having a large fortune tied up by the government, which if they only had your help they could access. They just need a tiny amount of money to get the proper documents executed, and they then will not only reimburse you but give you a large share of the freed funds.

This fairly sophisticated professional woman bought the whole story and sent the funds. Of course this was just the beginning. Once she was "hooked" there developed a constantly escalating need for money and complexity in recovering the "millions" tied up. I met her one day and she told me of helping this family in Africa that was pitiful and needed her help in getting their money. She really believed she was doing something good and her motivation was not primarily the possible return. She gradually gave what she had saved—$5,000—and then borrowed from her family, colleagues, and friends to give at least another $5,000. Unbelievable.

On the evening this girl told me the story of this family and how she is helping them get their money (and asked if maybe I could help) I told her straightaway that this sounded like the famous "Nigerian scam." No she said, it couldn't possibly be untrue. I went to my computer and for goodness sake there is even a Wiki article on it, which I showed her. She was stunned and started to cry. On the website was exactly the story she had been told. So now what? At that very moment they were pressing her for yet another sum that she had been working on giving them. I can't remember what exactly I told her to write them, asking for more information, but the result was she never heard back again.

Enter her family. After incredulously understanding how badly she had been duped they wanted to know how she was going to pay back her friends and others she had borrowed from to "help" the Nigerians. Needless to say the girl was humiliated and reluctant to come to terms with what she had done. "How could I be so stupid," she cried over and over. Nevertheless the family stepped in, her mother and sister. They paid off her debt to nonfamily members and let her pay back the family over an extended period. Her sister gave her a free apartment in which to live so she could begin saving again.

How does someone have a sister if China has a one-child policy? It turns out there are multiple exceptions not only to minorities but rural families. Indeed the one-child policy only really came into practice in 1979. According to the government only about one third of the families in China are actually subject to it. Hence it is easy for a thirty-year-old to have siblings who were born before the restrictions.

Another friend tells the story of hardships brought on for generations. Her family suffered retribution for two generations because her grandfather, like thousands of others, was an official in the Nationalist government of Chiang Kai-shek. The grandfather was sent by the Communists to be a farmer after having been a high government official, bringing suffering to the next generation because of the connection. Even today although there is no more retribution, there are memories.

Everywhere death comes calling to families, but its impact is amplified when multiple generations live together. It is especially poignant when a young member of the family dies. It is unexpected and very hard to reconcile. A friend's teenaged brother drowned when he jumped off the ferry to rescue his bookbag which had fallen over the side. Each year his sister Ping, now quite grown with a child of her own about her brother's age, returns to the same ferry and takes the crossing to Pudong just as her brother was doing when he drowned. She then takes a train to Nantong, a town about two hours from Shanghai on the north bank of the Yangtze River, to pray for his spirit.

When she arrives in Nantong she takes a tram up Lang Langshan (Wolf Hill), which leads to a Buddhist temple dedicated to a Song dynasty monk who was supposed to have had legendary powers over water demons. Even today sailors pray to him for protection on their voyages. There are multiple wooden temples and halls perched on the crest of the mountain. Ping prearranges her visit and over the years has gotten to know several of the monks who pray with her. After the formal ceremonies the ancient and wrinkled head monk appears and joins a luncheon the monastery has prepared for her and her son. She then reverses course back to Shanghai.

Having accompanied her on this ritual I must say I was impressed by the piety. I wonder how often this same kind of devotion would be found in our modern society in Western cultures? Maybe it would with the family of someone taken at such a young age, but from my limited experience I would say more often than not, after a year or so—especially with cremation—the rituals cease even if the memories linger.

On a happier note the early-morning grannies streaming out of housing complexes leading, carrying, pushing toddlers is quite charming. Off they go to the local parks and gather and watch chatting, ogling, cooing, and just having a delightful time with their grandchild.

An unexpected sight of tenderness came as I walked down the busy shopping street, Nanjing Xi Lu, with its consumers in droves hurrying along. I was stalled in my strolling by a young man, maybe thirty, holding his little child tucked in at his shoulder and tenderly and ever so unobtrusively, quietly singing a lovely song to his little sleeping bundle. It was as if no one else existed and I'm sure for him none did. I wouldn't have even noticed had I not had to slow down and ease past him.

# Chapter 17

## *Pollution and Epidemics*

In Chapter 13, I wrote about suspect food sources. Even more worrisome in China is the pollution, a topic that gets lots of press and, indeed, comment from those of us who live here. We now can check out an app that drives the government crazy because it gives the pollution levels for Beijing and Shanghai. It debuted last year and revealed the published statistics to be completely bogus. The data comes from the roof of the American legations. No one knows what the long-term effect of living with these pollution levels will have on all of our health. That's not to say anytime a sick citizen goes to the doctor the trip remains unnoticed; in fact every visit is carefully chronicled.

Everyone has their own pocket-sized booklet signed and stamped by the doctor that has their medical records written during each visit. When they finish a book a new one is started so that every time they visit a hospital they bring it and medical staff can page through and see what has been done and prescribed. It also serves as protection in case there is an error because it shows exactly what the doctor prescribed. My friend Candice Zeng had serious neck pain and went to Yue Yang Hospital. It happens to be two blocks from my home, so she asked me to accompany her; I did so willingly, not only to be of comfort to her but to see how the process worked.

Arriving at the entrance to the medical building there is a large open area and multiple reception counters where an ID Card is presented and payment of the equivalent of about $1 is made. The receptionist then gives a number and you proceed to an upstairs waiting area. A lighted board displays your number and you go in and see the doctor whose number matches yours. It is a small room with the doctor at a desk and a few chairs and an examining table. The patient relays his or her symptoms and like doctors the world over, the doctor says hmm, hmm, nods his or her head and scribbles a prescription. The patient then proceeds to a window and pays for the drugs and goes back downstairs where there are multiple windows. A screen displays the patient's number within a minute or two and the medication is handed over.

The Chinese doctors don't believe in treating pain; they think it keeps you attentive to solving your problem. In Candice's case, her pain is caused by being in front of a computer screen all day (she's an accountant). So part of the cure is to have her adjust her behavior and that's where the pain alerts her to adjust her posture, take more breaks, and raise the height of the screen. In addition the doctor had her go to a clinic that does acupuncture and administers small bottles that are filled with heat and stuck to your back. Supposedly these suck out bad humors but they leave a big black and blue mark. This is called cupping.[26] After ten sessions she tells me she is much better but not entirely cured of all pain.

I was not in Shanghai during the medical crisis of SARS, but I was in Singapore. It began with vague warnings that there was an unidentified virus that had caused the death of a Singapore resident who had recently traveled from Hong Kong. It evolved into an invisible plague that created empty streets, restaurants, and hotels.

Various sources have sorted out how it all began on February 21, 2003. Liu Jianlun, a sixty-four-year-old Chinese doctor who had treated cases in Guangdong arrived in Hong Kong to attend a wedding. He checked into the Metropole Hotel without apparent symptoms. But by the next day felt something was really wrong and went to the Kwong Wah Hospital, where he was admitted to the intensive-care unit. He died less than two weeks later on March 4.

It took weeks for the medical community to realize that this was something different and deadly. The virus was named the Severe Acute Respiratory Syndrome (SARS). Before it ended in Singapore, there were 238 people affected and 33 deaths. Worldwide there were 8,096 infected in 29 countries, and 774 deaths.[27] The numbers compared to the total population seem relatively small, but when you don't know what is causing it and people are dropping dead from it, there was general fear and apprehension. What should I do? Can I go to public places or should I just stay home? What if I am in the early stages? Does it float in the air? All these questions were on everyone's mind. As it crept through the country schools were closed. Theaters canceled performances.

During the epidemic one of the saddest moments for me was going to dinner at a friend's restaurant, and it was completely empty except for the owner and his wife all alone in a corner table. They had set up this restaurant at great expense only months before and now it was empty. It was financially devastating not only for them but for many in the service industry. Hotels had 20 percent occupancy, entertainment venues shut, restaurants and stores by schools and universities closed—even the ubiquitous food courts and kopitiams had few regulars. My friends at Ya Kun, one of the most famous Kaya toast and coffee joints, gave free breakfast and coffee to cabbies. Fear, courage, and generosity were all present. The emergency lasted for three intensive months, but gradually we, and the rest of the world, came out of it.

The Singapore government acted with speed, efficiency, and decisiveness. Just what you would want from a government at such a time. There are very few nations I would guess that could have acted so decisively. They told us all to take our temperature every day, twice and they sent everyone an electronic thermometer. (A rising fever was one of the early signs but of course not definitive.) Those who were suspected of developing SARS who had been exposed to a family member who had come down with it were quarantined to their homes. If they were found to have strayed they were fitted with an ankle bracelet that tracked their movements. If they still didn't obey they were thrown in jail. Medical workers who had roommates who worked in a different hospital were told to separate, and only those from the same hospital could room together. Cabbies were required to post in the cab their temperature twice a day. If they didn't their GPS was shut down and they couldn't get calls.

TV monitors were put in the airport that electronically took the temperature of everyone coming off a plane and displayed it in a little bubble above their image. If it was not normal they would be taken aside and examined by a doctor. Actually it was quite interesting to watch the screen as people passed. You also had to turn in a card as you left an aircraft telling the exact seat you were in and your address and phone number where you could be contacted in Singapore in case someone on the flight came down with SARS. Schools had been closed temporarily but on April 5, school closure was extended. This was over a month and a half after the first outbreak, and we were still in uncharted waters. The

Singapore government's work was smart, thorough, and complete, but not over.

I happened to know the head of immunology for the country. Throughout this time she would get on a worldwide telephone call with all the health institutes throughout the world and compare notes for what had transpired that day. Even the tiniest improvement in cases reported was encouraging. One of our Spirit of Enterprise awardees, who is a brilliant scientist, developed a test for identifying the virus. In some ways it was as if everyone was operating in a dark room groping for clues to what could be done both to identify the virus and to protect against it.

Early on the government, through a privately set up nonprofit initiative using the medical societies, started the Courage Fund, a fundraising drive created to highlight the courage of the health workers who were essentially flying blind in the beginning—not knowing how to protect themselves, how to identify real SARS patients and what exactly to do when they were identified. They hoped to raise a few million dollars to alleviate the costs to health workers and their families who either contracted SARS or who had a family member who did. (Most of the deaths in Singapore were health workers trying to save someone.) Instead of raising a few million dollars, Singaporeans opened their purses and wallets with unbelievable generosity and gave over $30 million. It was a tidal wave of concern from people who didn't normally give to charities as the government funded most social programs. I don't know anyone who declined to contribute, from my housekeeper to some of the wealthiest in the land.

When the Courage Fund had been set up it was intended for the 795 families who were affected by SARS, especially the medical workers. Over about two years about $2 million were expended for these purposes. This seemed to satisfy the purpose of the fund and time passed. So then what about the rest of the contributions? Instead of asking the contributors what should be done with it, including returning donations, the Courage Fund went on to give funding to a variety of projects, all probably worthwhile but not why we had all donated. For example, they created visiting professorships, bursary awards, healthcare humanity awards, and on and on.

A few years after SARS had passed I challenged the Courage Fund to return unused donations after all the criteria for fundraising had been met. The Médecins Sans Frontières (MSF, Doctors Without Borders) had done this after the great tsunami in 2004. This proved to be a good illustration of why Singapore's government needs more flexibility. I wrote the Courage Fund and had no response. I then wrote a minister who I knew and this elicited an invitation from the chairman of the fund to come and have tea. That's about all it was. A symbolic pat on the head, which really meant don't bother us.

Undeterred I went to a member of parliament who was also a doctor and the chairman of Raffles Medical, Dr. Loo Choon Yong. We had become friends when we worked on a government committee to suggest ways to improve Singapore. He is very connected to the leadership. He agreed with me and asked me to prepare a presentation that he could raise in parliament. I did and he did. We prepared an ironclad syllogism of why this entity shouldn't be using donors money the way they were. It was very critical but absolutely accurate. The minister overseeing the medical societies was upset and asked my member if I "was a troublemaker." I wish he had said yes, but he didn't.

I then called the press since it was a public session of parliament and gave them the story, which they reported the next day. A few days later my friend the doctor MP called me and said, "OK, that's enough; they get it." I have no doubt the prime minister sent that message. The end? No, the Courage Fund essentially has done nothing except be more transparent about what they are doing. That's Singapore. It will change though.

Along the lines of medicine in China I've had only very modest exposure. I signed up with an international hospital in Shanghai just so I would have a place to go in an emergency and have a very good Chinese doctor who was trained in America. I also have an official card for the local clinic a few blocks from my home. At this latter place I've had acupuncture and cupping to try and cure some back pain caused by herniated discs. Who knows if it helped or not, but I feel like a local with my card and health-record booklet. I've tried many things for my back, and it turns out that the best advice is from a Chinese doctor at St. Mary's in San Francisco. Do some specific back exercises. That seems to work.

26. Fire cupping is a treatment where a cotton ball dipped in 50 percent or greater alcohol is lit and the cotton ball is then introduced inside of the cup for a brief second. The cup is then placed on the patient. As a small vacuum has been created by the cooling of the hot air and gases inside the cup, the skin is drawn up into the cup creating a seal. If oil has been applied, the cups can be moved around the patient's body along the "meridians" and at specific points to allegedly help with immune boosting and other health benefits.

27. Health Promotion Board Singapore; US National Library of Medicine National Institutes of Health.

# Chapter 18

## Tale of the Three Pearls

When I'm with young people they give off a buzz, a feeling of becoming something both for themselves and their country. The idea that "China is on the way" is unspoken and never explicit but implied, as is "We're on the rise as other powers remain in place" (including the US). China is maybe even beginning to strut its stuff.

The young people I meet are very alert to the world around them and some of them know that they can get a superior advanced education in the United States, the United Kingdom, and Australia, as well as a few places like Singapore, which has a growing number of international graduate schools such as INSEAD, University of Chicago, and Yale.

There is a story told of Deng Xiaoping that at a meeting, not long after he assumed power, a lively discussion arose among the leaders as whether to let Chinese students go to America to study. Everyone at the meeting was against, saying, "They won't come home." Finally, Deng ended the meeting by saying, "If even one comes back it is worth it." Today most come back.

From time to time I am asked to write recommendation letters for Chinese students who want to go to graduate school in the United States. When talking to these students who are so eager to expand their horizons, I find they know more than I would have expected about the world around them and how other countries are governed. Even with a "walled" Internet they have all downloaded VPNs and scoot through the cyber wall.[28] There are certain things askew in the Chinese system, in one-party rule, but they see they are on an upward economic trajectory that is truly stunning and visible. All they have to do is consider their own family history to recognize that the best graduate education, and education means upward mobility, is still in the United States. Why wouldn't they want to go to NYU, Columbia, Chicago, Harvard, and so on?

I have written letters for Juquan Tiffany (王居荃), Xiaolei Echo (郭晓

蕾), Yue Yovia (许悦), and Lin Yi Sophie (程燚林). The first two went off to NYU, the other two University of Chicago and Birmingham in the United Kingdom. Some came from the farthest reaches of China without a dime, but lots of guts and talent, and all were bright, motivated young women.

These applicants have to compete with native speakers in a test that American students have taken for generations. They also must pass an English-proficiency test and file all the other regular application materials and in addition, most of them have to rely on scholarships, loans, and summer jobs. It is a tall mountain to climb but they do it.

This isn't just the case in China. Lan Nguyen, who ran the Spirit of Enterprise office in Vietnam, showed unbelievable moxie by breaking all the rules and going back to the American embassy in Hanoi repeatedly after being told she couldn't have a visa to attend a top American business school because "you won't come back." No matter what she said or showed of her links to Vietnam, family, job, husband, and little new daughter, the answer from young State Department officers was no. But they hadn't seen the likes of Lan. Against all the rules, she rescheduled herself for another interview and when she addressed the startled American Embassy official she said, "You have turned me down two times and here is why you should let me go." Thereupon she gave all her reasons. Contrary to what many officials would do, this official called in the two others who had interviewed her previously and asked why they had turned her down. Not hearing any compelling reason he issued her a visa then and there. No wonder she was sought after when she graduated. When the Embassy finds someone exceptional like Lan they should urge her to stay in the United States, not keep her out.

She went on to study at Thunderbird in Arizona, one of the outstanding graduate schools, where she focused entirely on international business. She was at the top of her class, graduated, and got a wonderful job at Coca-Cola in their corporate office in Atlanta, preparing her to return to Vietnam for a very important senior management position.

My experience with students in China has not been all about encouraging students to head off to the United States or the United Kingdom. In the last few years I've also spent a fair amount of time in Chinese graduate-level classes, talking to students. I've been to: Tsinghua University; the China Europe International Business School (CEIBS); East China Normal; Shanghai University of Finance and Economics; and

Shanghai Institute of Foreign Trade. I've also spoken at Global Sustainable Conference at the Shanghai Academy of Social Sciences and the Global Sustainable Leaders Forum in Beijing, and participated in the Thunderbird School of Global Management board's meeting with students. What has this added to my understanding of today's China? For one thing you meet some incredible people.

None of the students would do as well as they do without some inspirational teachers. It so happens that three I've met and worked with are each named Pearl—I've come to think of them as the Three Pearls.

Pearl Haoqing Wang of Shanghai Jiao Tong University is associate professor director at the Center for City, Creativity, and Communication and deputy director of Global Communication Research Institute. She was also a recent Rajawali fellow at Harvard's Kennedy School. But all these titles hardly capture what a wonderfully generous and creative soul she is. Pearl became a real help in the early days of the Spirit of Enterprise China as she agreed to the arduous task of editing the first two books on entrepreneurism launched by SOE. Both books of course are in Chinese and received wide circulation in bookstores and with readers interested in entrepreneurs.

The first book edited and enhanced by Pearl is entitled *Understanding Entrepreneurs* and is described in its summary as "a book about entrepreneurship in China." It's an edited version of nearly eighty interviews students conducted with entrepreneurs; they wrote these stories not only with their heads but with their hearts. Pearl wove it all together and brought out the key points entrepreneurs need to start a business, including their inspiration, actions, beliefs, the challenges of change, and never giving up.

I would prowl bookstores to see if it was in stock. Once when I was taking a photo of the book on the shelves an employee scolded me for taking photos. I then opened to the introduction of the book and showed her my name. What a transformation. She was so enthusiastic that she was meeting a writer who had a book in their store. It was heady. Needless to say I only wrote the introduction; Pearl put in the "heavy lifting" of writing, editing, and arranging the written student interviews that made up the book. I didn't try to explain this to the adoring clerk as I basked in the all-too-brief vainglory of recognition. Sorry, Pearl.

The second book, *The Power of Entrepreneurship*, was done in conjunction with the Communist Youth League of China, sort of the training wheels for those who hope to eventually be chosen to be members of the Communist Party. It was a harder task, with much more coordination with our partners. The "blurb" describes it this way: "This book is for the entrepreneurs and those who have a dream to start a business of their own. Included are the 140 entrepreneurs who were interviewed by 130 students from 20 Chinese universities. The entrepreneurs share their stories, experience, and spirit. They are realistic and their advice valuable. The Chinese entrepreneurs like the environment in China, full of vitality ... as the markets mature. From this book the reader can get to know the real life of the entrepreneur and be inspired to start their own business!" The Youth League's logo on the cover didn't hurt.

Not only did Pearl put in the work on the books but she also served on the board of governors of Spirit of Enterprise China as we tried to create a helpful and inspirational organization for China's youth. Time is always such a precious commodity and Pearl generously gave us all we needed. She continues to inspire students at Jiao Tong in Shanghai.

The second pearl is Pearl Tang Pei (沛 唐), an associate professor at Shanghai Institute of Foreign Trade, who introduced me not only to her large and interesting class but to her school's SIFE team. Students In Free Enterprise, recently rebranded as Enactus, describes itself as "an international nonprofit organization that works with leaders in business and higher education to mobilize university students to make a difference in their communities."

Less formally it is a group of students who create a project working on a business or social problem and bring new solutions to it. Every participating campus at the end of the school year competes in a "World Cup" to choose the most successful team project. My group turned out to be the toast of China as they competed with thousands of students and hundreds of other universities and came in third in all of China.

I am doubly pleased that they allowed me to help as a patron-advisor for their project. Student leader Rose Zhao (赵婷婷) focused the group on addressing two social problems: that of air pollution from straw burning, and the farmer's low income derived from their crop. They convinced local farmers to stop burning straw and to turn the straw into purchasable tourist items such as sandals. The team showed an intelligent way to simultaneously reduce air pollution and raise the farmer's income. Through glimpses and snatches of stories they told me I also got the impression they had a lot of fun as well. We had a celebratory party in my home after their success in Beijing, featuring lots of beer and laughter. These good kids provide a glimpse of future China.

My final pearl is Pearl Donghui Mao of Tsinghua University. For seven years she was the executive director of the MBA program, School of Economics and Management, and recently took the challenge of a new initiative at Tsinghua called the x-lab, which will focus on entrepreneurship and new venture development. My expectation is that it will be a successful incubator for new business creativity.

While running the MBA program she managed to inspire students who came from all over the world to get their MBA at Tsinghua. The program gathered people of many cultures, backgrounds, and languages together for brilliant academics. The students must acclimate themselves to a new environment as well as their courses. The classes are all taught in English, the international language of business, air traffic, and diplomacy.

On the day I gave my lecture some students arranged a dinner for me. The students laughed about that it wasn't only academics they had to conquer but they also had to figure out how to live in a Chinese apartment house, buy food, and get around. This wasn't just international students; it was those from China who had never lived on their own. I know the feeling!

Tsinghua (清华大学) in Beijing is a dream school for many students and generally considered to be the #1 university in China. There are competitive exams held on one day all over China for high-school seniors and if they score high enough, are from the right provincial region, and have specifically indicated that they wish to go to this school only, then they have something like a one hundred to four million shot at getting in. The current system of selection makes the students pre-choose where they want to go before the test. If they don't score high enough to get into the university they have targeted they are assigned one by the government. (Lately there has been some talk about changing the system, and at least one university is now choosing its own students.)

My friend Xiaoxiao Zhang had a score high enough to get into Peking University (which also vies for the #1 spot and is one of the top four along with Tsinghua, Fudan, and Jiao Tong), but she targeted Fudan and went there successfully. Fortunately for me she majored in Chinese literature and revised my English introduction written for our SOE first book and turned it into such good Chinese that people thought I was a native. My original text had a few quotes, which she duly got rid of replacing them with "more contemporary" ones (ah, to be young again).

At Tsinghua I rode my shaky bicycle (me, not the bike) around the campus with two students who had rented it for me so they could show me the very extensive and beautiful grounds. It is a big deal to be part of this community. The campus is huge and even spending about an hour cycling around we didn't even come close to covering all the winding paths, lakes, and noble buildings. There is one that resembles MIT's iconic building and with good reason. Very early on, MIT developed a relationship with Tsinghua that persists today. In an odd historical and not exactly honorable moment, the Qing Dynasty gave reparations to the Western countries that had invaded Beijing in 1901. This was a sort of aftermath of the Opium Wars of the mid-1800s and redux of the 1860 sacking of the Summer Palace. The Qing were obliged to pay over monies for the destruction caused by the Boxers to the foreign legations.[29] (Nothing was said about the destruction caused after by the invading Westerners.) The payments were made to the various allied powers but in a stroke of brilliance Teddy Roosevelt said the United States would not accept the payment, had it reduced, and instructed that it should be directed to scholarships for Chinese students, which in turn led to the founding of Tsinghua.

I was asked back toward the end of the school year to deliver the commencement address to the MBA students but was unable to do it due to a prior commitment. Hopefully another time.

**28.** VPN is a Virtual Private Network that when downloaded makes your computer appear to be some place other than where it is. In China it is used to get around the censors so you can access Facebook, YouTube, Yahoo, and other sites that are blocked.
**29.** The Boxer Rebellion, also known as Boxer Uprising or Yihetuan Movement, was a protonationalist movement by the "Righteous Harmony Society" in China between 1898 and 1901, opposing foreign imperialism and Christianity.

# Chapter 19

## *Social Enterprises and Nonprofits*

A student interviewed me once and asked, where did I get the idea of "helping others"?

My answer was that I supposed it came from my own family. We learned many lessons at the evening dinner table. Schools drummed into us that we had to consider others as well as ourselves. I distinctly remember in elementary school we were told by the nuns to finish all of our lunch because there were "poor, starving children in Europe." We also put small coins in cardboard banks for the "pagan babies." In China, that idea has evolved in interesting ways.

For starters, I became an investor in a women's fashion boutique. Strange, yes, except it has a charity component. NuoMi is a women's boutique that combines the selling of upmarket clothes with trying to create enhanced lifestyle opportunities for very poor families, often with members who are impaired in some way. The whole idea is to build a business that generates enough profit to help the disadvantaged. The company line is that NuoMi has "Japanese production standards, American designs, and Chinese-style management." That's very funny although not entirely inaccurate.

I was talked into this investment by an old friend whom I had known in Singapore. She is a very devout Buddhist and lured me into the investment by showing how this model of a social entrepreneur is on the leading edge of transformation in society. It makes a lot of sense in theory, and for those who know how to execute effectively (like my friend Geoff Woolley of Unitus Impact),[30] it can be extremely lucrative and beneficial to both investors and the underprivileged.

I was especially impressed with the founder of NuoMi, Bonita Lim, a woman with an expansive heart and a clear business vision. She'd use recurring cash flow from the business to help the less fortunate and build the business. Yet within months a pleading call for capital arrived. Huh? I later realized Bonita's guru on finance and strategy had little real operating experience. She was good at numbers but the strategy offered was to open twenty stores as fast as possible, because that was what was needed to cover the costs of the office production and design. People with business experience would counsel that you needed to get costs under control first; then you wouldn't have to rely on some illusionary future cash flow to cover the basics.

As investors know it takes time to get operating strategy and operations right and only then should expansion follow. Early on there was high staff turnover—they were good people but often didn't understand the idealist objectives of the whole effort. Changing designs and slow customer pay were also problems that had to be overcome by the indomitable spirit of Bonita and a core group of "believers."

Recently Bonita is thinking that franchising might be an additional way to succeed. Her brother in Canada is very successful at that. This happens to be something I know a lot about, having established an insurance franchise company more than thirty years ago that today still thrives.[31] Hopefully this enhances the whole enterprise, not like a rocking horse, which has plenty of action but not much progress. Gradually she is sorting out the best corporate organizational approach and will probably separate the operating divisions from the charitable umbrella by forming a foundation.

This brings up another issue which I hope isn't just personal pique. Despite suggesting over and again that Bonita could use a board of experienced people she has never once asked for my advice. My own experience is solid; it comes from creating an international boutique investment bank and two investment funds with corporate investors that are some of the world's largest financial institutions. On the other hand my advice may be lousy. What do I know about running a fashion business? There are several possible explanations. One is that Bonita's husband, who is a management consultant, is possibly her main source of business advice. If so, I won't suggest getting a new husband, since he is a wonderful father to four stepchildren, but I would say you'd better find a broad array of experienced advisors.

I have an option to convert my note into NuoMi stock when additional investors come after mine, and thankfully Bonita's dad, an extremely successful and savvy businessman, stepped forward to help.

All does not diminish what NuoMi is and will be. Any business starting has these same kind of problems, especially with cash flow. Indeed tight cash flow is often a sign not of a failing strategy, but growing *success* putting strains on existing capital. NuoMi has not yet had its fifth birthday and when we used to create or finance new companies we often would project losses into the fifth year. It takes time to work things out and generate recurring profits. Some of the biggest names in current business such as Google and Facebook took years. China's largest online business site, Baidu, is said to still not be profitable after many years of spectacular growth.

In the meantime I bring anyone who is interested in fashion to the nearest store. It is great to show off the lovely offerings and point out the families we are helping.

I've gotten involved in another start up nonprofit called ZenPlay (www.zenplay.org). It is the original idea of Mari Kawawa in San Francisco who, along with taking care of five children and her husband Patrick, has other ventures and is extraordinarily generous. She has engaged some enthusiastic friends to start a new nonprofit to help out children's charities. The concept is to use new technology and social media to raise funds for children's charities.

Having signed up to participate I thought that maybe we could do something innovative using today's interest in apps and online games. I am reluctant to admit that I am an Angry Birdsaholic and avid user of Tencent's new game TIMi and am forced to play a game or two every few days. As my mother used to say, "Little things amuse little minds." She was right.

For some innovation I went to Lan Haiwen of UltiZen (www.ultizen.com) or as they proclaim on their website: "UltiZen Games is China's largest all-platform game art–outsourcing partner and PC-game developer for many of the most respected games companies around the world." It was started by the very innovative and persistent Lan, whom, as you have already read, I had gotten to know through the Spirit of Enterprise. One of their most popular is Zombie Neighborhood! Who doesn't play games on their phone or iPad or Android? I do and so do millions of people around the world. Our meeting turned out to be fortuitous for several reasons, not just reaffirming that we found an ideal role model for the students but also because he turned out to be an enthusiastic promoter of ZenPlay. He took the idea of having telephone apps and asked if UltiZen would create some for us.

Not only did Lan like the idea he embellished it by saying they would create some games exclusively for us, launch them on iPhones, iPads, and Androids, help us market them, take all the revenues derived, and direct them to the children's charities we designated. Not only that, he said they would pay all taxes associated with the income and give us the gross, not the net. They would maintain the games on their servers and post all funds received on their website for all to see. Furthermore, rather unbelievably, he would let any game distributer in any country take the game and translate it into their own language, plus he would introduce us to other game companies in China to try and get them to participate. How is that for enthusiasm?

One amusing result is that I'm learning about games and objects. I'm learning to let the players experience on- and offline opportunities, both individually and collectively. I'm actually learning about the online-game business. For example, objects that help you improve your abilities can generate income. If someone chooses the option "drink from this vessel and you can have added powers" then we can hope to charge a few yuan for the gulp.

Recurring income is the Golden Fleece of nonprofits. We all dream of a way to create a flow of "donor" funds instead of having to constantly going hat-in-hand to foundations and individuals for single- or multiple-year donations. Together we cooked up a plan that UltiZen would create at least one game and it would be a free download but in the game would be "objects" that the player could pay to use to increase their capability while playing the game.

Why suggest the funds come directly to ZenPlay to dispense? In China to become an approved nonprofit you have to jump through many hoops that end up nowhere until you are tucked within one of the government entities who will then take at least 5 percent for administration. By having UltiZen dispense the funds we achieve the result for our charities and don't even have to form a nonprofit. In the meantime we will identify some well-run children's charities and after some due diligence put them in rotation for receiving funds. At some point, when it is felt they have received enough, they will rotate off our list and new ones will come on. Because of some market difficulties UltiZen has had to delay its creations for us but I have high hopes that in time they will.

So far all our efforts are with volunteers but at the same time Mari is working on some foundations to get operating funds in America where we have formed a tax-free 501(c)(3). We are also working in Japan to duplicate the efforts and through a fundraiser organized by Mari have been able to make our first donation to an orphanage in Japan.

As when I started Spirit of Enterprise, the first to step up and help was Tan Kin Lian, the former CEO of NTUC Income in Singapore, who, imbued with the entrepreneurial spirit, started his own game company when he retired from the insurance company. When I explained our ZenPlay concept to him he immediately gave us a game called Bright Words. This can be downloaded into any iPhone. It is designed to help high-school students expand their English vocabulary especially in preparation for university entrance exams.

One of the charities that we've identified is Stepping Stones, a not-for-profit charitable organization with a mission to improve the education and general welfare of disadvantaged children in China. Stepping Stones works with expatriate and local Chinese volunteers to teach English in Shanghai's migrant schools and community centers and recruits, trains, coordinates, and supports around two hundred volunteers to teach four thousand students in fifteen migrant schools and community centers in Shanghai.

I traveled with Stepping Stones to visit some schools in Henan Province, a nearly six-hour train ride from Shanghai. This is a very poor province and the villages we visited, Zhao Zhuang (张庄村) and Tian Fu Yuan in Zhangqiao Township, are small villages with mud brick homes and dirt roads. This is not the image the world has of modern China, but many hundreds of millions still live in these small, backward places.

We broke into two groups and I was assigned to Zhao Zhuang village school. The village itself was like what I had seen in photos depicting rural China—but maybe a century ago.

The entire village is surrounded by fields. The houses mostly had high walls and elegant central doors, almost all closed. When you could peek into a courtyard, most of the houses were one story. Here and there was a two-story structure that was more modern and not made from mud bricks, and there was renovation and construction going on throughout the village, some of it additions, some of it reinforcing homes. From my perspective, although there was work going on there didn't seem to be any signs of prosperity. I only saw one car and it was just passing through.

The lanes were mostly packed dirt and only one cart or bicycle could easily pass along. Even the main village road from the nearby motorway was so narrow our van had to constantly almost stop to let carts from the opposite direction navigate slowly past us. At one point our driver had to get out and with a long stick prop up a wire set across the road that was too low for a modern vehicle to pass. One very obstinate and irritated farmer had laid his water pipe across the road so he could water his field, completely disregarding passing traffic. We slowly ran over the malleable pipe as he complained mightily that we would break it. Later on return trip he had erected almost a barricade of eight-foot dried corn stalks covering the pipe. Our driver removed some so we could pass as the farmer glared from the sidelines. Eventually he partially buried the pipe by digging a ditch across the road. I wonder if he filled it in when he was finished irrigating his field of grain?

Piled everywhere in the town were very high heaps of dried corn stalks, the last crop to come out of the fields. We were told they were used for fires and that parts of the stalks were woven into long rope-like strands by some of the local ladies as they sat on their front stoop. I saw one baby and one young woman who happened to be the mother, but every other occupant of the village was old and weather-beaten. This is what is happening all over China; the young flee the villages because there is no work and they don't want to be farmers tending one plot all the rest of their lives. Twenty-five percent of Shanghai's population has migrated to the city from places like this.

With twelve other volunteers in two teams, we taught classes in two schools from kindergarten to sixth grade for four days. I was with a lead experienced teacher from Stepping Stones, Karen Chow, and we held forth with a class of thirty-five third graders. The students were wonderful. They were very forthcoming and happy to participate with their temporary teachers. The children learn English, beginning in the very early grades, and our little class performed very well when we went through colors, some common objects like a desk, pen, and similar everyday items. We colored, played games, and sang. "Hello, hello, I am fine, how are you? I am fine, how are you." Their songs were so full throated and happy.

All the children are from the village and run home for lunch. They are known as "left-behind" children because for the most part their parents are in some far-off city making money. They are taken care of by their grannies or a close relative. One little boy with rosy cheeks stayed behind in the classroom after all the kids had rushed home for lunch. He told us that "My Mom's not home so I will stay here." He had a little fruit bar that he carefully unwrapped and silently ate as he looked out the window at the schoolyard where a few children remained playing. He was dear and sad.

Often as I would leave the classroom at the beginning of a short recess a little girl or boy would silently grasp my hand and walk down the stairs hand-in-hand to the play yard. They did this without asking, as if they instinctively felt you were there to take care of them. I was so touched by their openness and love. In the play yard during recess the kids would swarm around you and just smile and seem to want be with us. They couldn't communicate with English sentences but really did communicate with their eyes and pulled on my sleeve to show me a pen or some little object they had. Several on the last day gave me string necklaces with colored beads. I wore them with great pride.

Each day at the end of the school day there would be dozens of old people standing outside the school gates to pick up their little one. These people looked very sun baked, in dull but warm clothes, and their hard life was reflected in their features, deeply lined. Their teeth were almost universally bad. They seemed kind and anxiously awaited their charges.

I felt so sad when we had to leave after such a short visit and wondered what would become of these children without any parental guidance. Maybe the grannies do a good job and all will be well, but how could you not be moved as several of our third graders ran out of the school to our van and stood at the door silently crying with pleading eyes as we got ready to depart? I wanted to jump out and just scoop them up and take them away to a better life.

On the Shanghai news I saw a sad story about a child left with relatives. A five-year-old who was brought up in a village by her grandparents was returned to the parents in the city. This little girl didn't know her real parents and they were strangers to her. Like many families they lived in an apartment building, and when her parents had gone to work the child wandered by herself into the neighborhood, just as she had in her village. Soon a watchful neighborhood policeman spotted her and when asked her father's name, she didn't know it, she only knew her grannie's name. Sad but understandable. Not long after her father came looking for her and they were reunited.

An acquaintance of mine teaches in a mountainous area south of Xi'an, the city famous for the terra-cotta warriors. She says in her village area the houses are usually four rooms with the privy and kitchen outside the main building. In her school the classes have fifty students per class. Some of the students live too far from their villages and have to spend the whole week boarding at the school.

She says in teaching English they really just teach to the test the government mandates. These tests are important for the future of the children because the outcome can determine the quality of their next school. The kids learn to pass the test, not to speak English. This is reinforced by the fact that this girl's English is atrocious yet she is an English teacher. She grew up in a rural area and when she was a teenager had a relationship with a married man, which produced a now-eight-year-old girl. Her own life reflects the many hardships that have to be overcome to escape village life.

Another one of the charities we're hoping to help is the Child Hope Relief Foundation Children's Hope Foundation (www.childrenshope.org.cn), a local nonprofit specializing in the rescue of orphans and disadvantaged children, especially after a disaster like the Sichuan earthquake and the one in Qinghai in 2010. They have also been trying to persuade the National People's Congress and the CPPCC National Committee to call for the establishment of universal medical insurance for children.

Then there is Shanghai Qing Cong Quan Children's Intelligence Training Center (www.qingcongquan.org.cn), which does professional rehabilitation training and counseling for children with autism and other developmental disorders.

We've also identified Qinghai Gesang Hua (www.gesanghua.org), located in the sparsely populated far west, in the Hainan Tibetan Autonomous Prefecture. This new organization provides financial assistance to youngsters to complete their studies with one-on-one funded scholarship programs. They also help shore up the infrastructure of schools.

As you can imagine there are worthy organizations involved in every possible aspect of helping children. Shanghai dazzles us by the glowing modernity of Pudong and the incredible infrastructure (the city will have twenty-one subway lines by 2020), its many new museums, the number of bridges being built, and fast trains racing along. But behind all the dazzle are six million migrants in Shanghai, many who are the parents of the "left-behind" children. The Shanghai social services organizations try and cope but it is realistically impossible to provide schooling, shelter, health care for the remaining seventeen million residents with Hukous, the household registration system, that entitles them to local services. It isn't just migrants who strain the system.

As with any large metropolitan area, no matter how sleek—even as sleek as Singapore—there will always be folks who can't cope. A term often used for them in the United States is those who "fall between the cracks." I hate the saying because it absolves those who are supposed to be alert in social services not to admit responsibility.

So what are the results of this overworked and inadequate system? Everything you can think of, including babies abandoned in garbage pails, cripples banging their heads on the pavement begging for a few *quai* from passersby, housing units without indoor plumbing, jammed clinics, and on and on. So there are many, many nonprofits addressing all these needs, and the government, while encouraging their participation at the same time looks askance at their growing prominence. Control is a very big deal to the Communist Party; hence local governments are pulled between encouraging nonprofits and controlling or, when possible, preempting their activities.

An illustration of this, in 2011 a prominent journalist from *Phoenix Weekly* magazine, Deng Fei, paid a visit to very poor and rural southwest Guizhou province, where he saw that the students didn't even have a school cafeteria. He went on Sina Weibo (which is like Twitter and Facebook, two American social sites that are blocked in China), pointed out the problem and asked for help. He has generated more than two million followers, many who have donated to his charity Free Lunch for Children.[32] Deng says almost one million of those people have helped more than 160 schools and 25,000 children.

Many of the undernourished are those "left-behind" children. One estimate says there are over twenty-six million youngsters who do not have a good meal all day. According to another study, these kids are maturing at heights of up to six inches shorter than the average properly fed Chinese child. Many of the "left-behind" kids have no one to help them with their homework, because their guardians, often a grandparent, haven't had proper schooling themselves.

After a little more than a year of successful efforts by Free Lunch for Children, the central government in Beijing has stepped in and announced it will start a nutritional subsidy program for all of China's primary and junior-high students in rural areas. The National Development and Reform Commission announced they will put up ¥16 billion for a program of rural nutrition. If Deng is right it costs only ¥3 per student which would be ¥78 million needed every year.[33] So what's the difference in taking care of twenty-six million students? If the government statistic I have is correct then it is more than two hundred times Deng's amount. Is the extra ¥15.9 billion for administration? Surely there can be better meals for these children, can't there?

Even if all my numbers are cockeyed, the message is plain from the government. *We are going to muscle into this arena and we will solve the problem.* Further message: There will be a lot of money coming into the provinces and school districts and schools. None of whom have to account to the public for spending it. Could some of it seep into regional officials' pockets? Is the Pope a Catholic?

Things like this discourage some good people, but not Deng, who will no doubt keep his program going and keep the spending as transparent as he does today. He has a very ingenious system of oversight from former officials and a wide array of Weibo donors and followers who are keeping an ever-vigilant eye on each school and how they handle the funds and the quality of the meals being served. Each school must post in detail on the web the exact expenditure for each food item and the totals. If they misreport, they lose their funding.

Along the lines of being discouraged with how government officials administer nonprofits there was a notorious case of a very flashy young woman, Ms. Guo, whose blog included pictures of her new Maserati and fancy clothes. Yet she worked for the Red Cross Society of China. It caused a storm of outrage. How could a nonprofit worker be so wealthy? The Red Cross at first denied she worked for them but then amended that to say she worked in one of the multiple for profit companies that they had created to do its work. For profit companies; who are they? The plot thickened. She got the car and money from one of the officers who was allegedly having an affair with her. Well, how did *he* get the money? More complications. The Red Cross Society of China isn't the Red Cross as we know it at all. Just the name is the same and it isn't affiliated with the International Red Cross. After a few more press releases, he quit and she was trashed by netizens.

It is said the Red Cross revenues have dropped by more than 75 percent although they don't share details. It is hard enough to get donors to give to legitimate organizations like Lunch for Children but scandals like this make everyone pull back in mistrust when personal giving is just in its infancy.

This explains why at ZenPlay we are trying to create new ways to generate funds for good causes. It is going to take a lot of change to get the savvy Chinese consumer to place their trust in nonprofit organizations they don't know well.

**30.** Unitus Impact (http://unitusimpact.com) is an early-stage impact-investing firm with the mission of improving the livelihoods of low-income populations by supporting the growth of scalable, financially attractive livelihood ventures.
**31.** The ISU Group of Companies (www.isugroup.com) is a privately owned independent insurance and financial firm with 100 offices in the USA.
**32.** http://mianfeiwucan.tmall.com or www.51give.org; click Free Lunch for Children.
**33.** As of October 2013, ¥78 million is US $12.7 million; ¥15.1 billion is US $2.5 billion.

## *And Now What?*

I would like to finish by reiterating a quote with which I began, "What does anybody here know of China?... Everything is covered by a veil, through which a glimpse of what is within may occasionally be caught, a glimpse just sufficient to set the imagination at work and more likely to mislead than to inform."

I hope I have done more informing than misleading, but I understand that I only have glimpses, my Shanghai world—nurturing, interesting, and confusing—all the time adding to the tapestry of an interesting life but still only a speck of what is going on every day in this vibrant and fascinating country.

Foreigners, including me, are routinely asked, "How long have you been here; how long will you stay?" My answer is that as long as I have something to share that might ever-so-slightly improve someone's life. As long as I have the spirit, health, friendships, and can keep learning, enjoying and contributing then you'll find me here. Or maybe not.

Shanghai,
Datian Lu, 2013

## Further Reading

I've read or wandered through all of the following books and think they broadened my understanding of China. No doubt I'm missing some great ones but here's where I am now, and you may want to follow.

Anything Prof. John K. Fairbanks writes needs to be read thoughtfully, such as his *China: A New History*. Other valuable books, Jonathan D. Spence's *Search for Modern China* and *To Change China*; Henry Kissinger, *On China*; and books like Simon Winchester's *The Man Who Loved China* about Cambridge professor Joseph Needham are all thoughtful and revealing. Even *On a Chinese Screen* by Somerset Maugham gives a glimpse in every chapter of a different situation or an insightful meeting.

I've struggled though some of the "must-reads" like *Call to Arms* by Lu Xun, *Dream of the Red Chamber* by Cao Xueqin (only two of the four volumes), as well as the poems of Bai Juyi and the annoying and pedantic *Fortress Besieged* by Zhongshu Qian.

The books that impressed me most and taught me so much about contemporary China very often are novels. Local Fudan professor Anyi Wang's *The Song of Everlasting Sorrow*; *Brothers*, *To Live*, *Chronicle of a Blood Merchant* and *China in Ten Words* by Yu Hua. *Big Breasts Wide Hips* by Nobel laureate Yan Mo.

I got a real sense of the '30s and '40s from *Love in a Fallen City* by Eileen Chang or the much earlier *The Sing-Song Girls of Shanghai* translated by her, but written by Han Bangqing. I even went to the Paramount ballroom one night to see what the old atmosphere might be like. You can also find some of the same atmosphere in the dining room of the old Jin Jiang and the restored ballroom in the Garden Hotel on MaoMing.

Also helpful: *Life and Death in Shanghai* by Nien Cheng; *My China Years* and *Inside Red China* by Helen Foster Snow; *Opium War* by Julia Lovell; *River Town: Two Years on the Yangtze* and *Oracle Bones* by Peter Hessler.

*Mao: The Unknown Story* by Jung Chang and Jon Halliday; *The Private Life of Chairman Mao* by Li Zhi-Sui; *Quotations from Chairman Mao Tse-Tung* (the little red book). *The Kissinger Transcripts: The Top Secret Talks with Beijing and Moscow*, edited by William Burr.

*A Jesuit in the Forbidden City: Matteo Ricci 1552–1610* by R. Po-chia Hsia; *Journey to the East: the Jesuit Mission to China 1579–1724* by Liam Matthew Brockey; *The Memory Palace of Matteo Ricci* by Jonathan D. Spence; *Following the Footsteps of the Jesuits in Beijing* by Thierry Meynard, S.J.

*A Year in Tibet* by Sun Shuyun; *Restless Empire* by Odd Westad; *Midnight in Peking* by Paul French. *The Plum in the Golden Vase or, Chin P'ing Mei: Volume Four: The Climax*, translated by David Tod Roy; *China Watcher: Confessions of a Peking Tom* by Richard Baum; *Stilwell and the American Experience in China, 1911–1945* by Barbara Tuchman.

*The Opium War: Drugs, Dreams, and the Making of China* by Julia Lovell; *Leave Me Alone: A Novel of Chengdu* by Xuecun Murong; *China Airborne* by James Fallows; *Soul Mountain* by Gao Xingjian. *Empire of the Summer Moon* by S. C. Gwynne; *Tide Players: The Movers and Shakers of a Rising China* by Zha Jianying; *Inside the Red Mansion: On the Trail of China's Most Wanted Man* by Oliver August.

*Three Sisters* by Bi Feiyu; *Wild Swans: Three Daughters of China* by Jung Chang; *China Road: A Journey into the Future of a Rising Power* by Bob Gifford; *Shanghai Girls* by Lisa See; *Mr. China: A Memoir* by Tim Clissold; *Tales of Old Shanghai* by Graham Earnshaw; *Shanghai Boy, Shanghai Girl* by George Wang; *Oh Shanghai: Gangsters in Paradise* by Lynn Pan; and Amy Tan's *The Bonesetter's Daughter*, *The Kitchen God's Wife* and *The Joy Luck Club*.

Finally, I even dipped into cooking with *China Modern: 100 Cutting-Edge, Fusion-Style Recipes for the 21st Century* by Ching-He Huang.

**Russell R. Miller** is a native of San Francisco, California, and has been working on projects in Asia for almost thirty years. With headquarter offices in Hong Kong and Singapore, he directed two investment funds and in 2002 founded The Spirit of Enterprise, a nonprofit, cultural, educational organization dedicated to fostering the entrepreneurial spirit. Recently, he joined with others to start ZenPlay, a nonprofit aiming to help children's charities.

He also worked for three years in the US Congress in Washington, DC, and won a contested nomination for a US congressional seat, although he lost the general election. His papers for that period are found in the Bancroft Library at the University of California, Berkeley, a principal repository library for California history.

Prior to living in Singapore and now in Shanghai, he was an investment banker, having created a specialty firm in the United States that focused on the domestic and international insurance industry. He founded the National Insurance Leadership Symposium, a leadership forum for insurance executives. He served as a trustee and executive committee member of the College of Insurance, St. John's University, in New York. He was a cofounder of the Insurance Industry Charitable Fund. A recipient of The Republic of Singapore's Pingat Bakti Masyarakat Public Service Medal, he lives in both Shanghai and San Francisco.

Additional copies of this paperback edition of
*An American in Shanghai* may be ordered from Amazon.com

www.ingramcontent.com/pod-product-compliance
Lightning Source LLC
Chambersburg PA
CBHW061310110426
42742CB00012BA/2127